Ballet Old and New

Ballet
Old and New

by ANDRÉ
LEVINSON

*Translated from the Russian
by Susan Cook Summer*

DANCE HORIZONS • NEW YORK

ISBN 0-87127-130-3

Library of Congress Catalog Card Number 81-70095

Printed in the United States of America

Dance Horizons, 1801 East 26th Street, Brooklyn, N.Y. 11229

The decorations used throughout this book
are from the 1918 Russian edition.

Cover and interior design by Bert Waggott

1 2 3 4 5 6 7 8 9 10

Contents

v

Introduction

S T. P E T E R S B U R G was a city of extremes and paradoxes during the last decade of the nineteenth century. Realism, which had dominated cultural life since the 1860s, was being challenged by Symbolism, an "other-worldly" trend which sought to transcend reality and evoke mystical feelings through imagery. Besides Symbolism, the rejection of Realism brought in its wake heightened interest in Western civilization on the one hand, and in the traditions of Old Russia on the other, which last, often called the Neo-Nationalist movement, was further supported by the art colonies of Savva Mamontov and Princess Tenisheva. This whole era of contrasts was typified in Diaghilev's journal *Mir Iskusstva* (1899–1904) on whose pages all the leading aesthetes—artists, writers, critics—of the time carried on their endless debates.

Andrei Yakovlevich Levinson was born into this world of artistic ferment in 1887. Living near the famed Maryinsky Theater, he watched an endless stream of dancers and musicians going to and from rehearsals and performances. And it was there at the Maryinsky that at the age of about five Levinson experienced a *coup de foudre* during a performance of *The Sleeping Beauty*. Perhaps his life-long passion for the classical ballet stemmed from this very experience, a passion which led him into a career that earned him the reputation of Europe's finest dance critic and Diaghilev's chief opponent.

Levinson's first book appeared at approximately the time he graduated from the Imperial University in St. Petersburg where he studied psychology, philosophy, philology, Greek, Latin, Romance languages and history of art. What was to become an amazingly prolific writing career began in 1908 with a modest volume devoted to the Finnish painter Axel Gallen.

The next year, as Diaghilev opened his first Saison Russe in Paris, Levinson began to contribute ballet reviews to *Apollon,* Makovsky's elegant, aristocratic journal, and to *Rech'*, where his landmark critiques of the Ballets Russes were to appear. In his distinctively forceful, often ironic style, Levinson expressed his disapproval of Diaghilev's subordination of dance to costumes, decor and music. Time and again he voiced his fear that Diaghilev was damaging choreography's classical foundation for the sake of novelty. Nor was Diaghilev his only target. Levinson's reviews of music hall performances, Negro and Oriental dancing, and modern dancers such as Loie Fuller and Isadora Duncan all reaffirmed his belief that the classical technique was the only foundation upon which dance could develop into a self-sufficient art form.

In 1913 Levinson joined the faculty of the Imperial University of St. Petersburg as a professor of French literature and translated a series of French writers, including Stéphane Mallarmé and André Gide, into Russian. The following year his first book on ballet, *Mastera baleta,* was published. This was a set of historical essays on Jean-Georges Noverre, Salvatore Viganò, Auguste Vestris and Carlo Blasis. His next book, the present *Staryi i novyi balet* (1918), comprised six of his most important articles on the dance. Nowhere else does Levinson so powerfully oppose Diaghilev's innovations or so pointedly express his distaste for Igor Stravinsky's "barbaric" music. While the articles focused on Diaghilev's Saisons Russes, Levinson also discussed Isadora Duncan's appearances in Russia and a variety of aesthetic issues. Published in 1918, it was his last work to appear in Russia.

The next year, fleeing the Revolution, he went to Lithuania with his wife and child. After traveling through Germany and Siberia, he arrived in 1921 in Paris with a copy of *Les liaisons dangereuses* tucked under his arm. It did not take Levinson long to establish himself as a vital force in French dance, literary and artistic circles.

Paris in the twenties was teeming with creative energy of every conceivable kind. By this time Diaghilev's company had abandoned its earlier Russian-Eastern themes *(Cleopatra, Sheherazade, Prince Igor)* in favor of the sophisticated modernism of *Les Biches, Le*

Train Bleu and *La Pastorale,* and the neo-classicism of *The Sleeping Beauty* and *Ode.* The active Russian emigré community in Paris included celebrated painters, musicians and writers such as Bunin, Remizov, Tsvetaeva and Merezhkovsky.

Levinson joined the faculty of the Sorbonne, where he taught Russian literature, and began writing for leading French and Russian publications. His articles appeared in *La Revue musicale* and *Candide, Nouvelles littéraires* and *Le Temps, Sovremennye zapiski* and the Berlin-based *Zhar-Ptitsa.* In 1922 Georges Casella of *Comoedia* invited Levinson to become one of the magazine's chief critics. Upon Levinson's acceptance he remarked, "I certainly hope you'll get rid of *pointes,* tutus and all the old opera stuff!" *"Mon cher patron,"* Levinson replied, "with your kind permission, I shall do precisely the opposite." The same year, 1922, the first of his books on Leon Bakst appeared. This was followed by *La Danse au théâtre* in 1924, a collection of literary essays, *Croisières,* in 1927, and a book of articles devoted to American writers (among them Theodore Dreiser, Eugene O'Neill and Sinclair Lewis) in 1929. It was also in 1929 that the two books by which Levinson is best known today were published: his biography of Marie Taglioni and *La Danse d'aujourd'hui,* a volume that covers the Ballets Russes, Anna Pavlova, Isadora Duncan, La Argentina and many types of exotic dancing. Often forgotten is the fact that at the same time he contributed dozens of articles to British and American publications, particularly New York's *Theatre Arts Monthly.*

In 1927 Levinson was awarded the Légion d'Honneur and in 1932, a year before his death, he became a naturalized French citizen. His last work to appear during his lifetime was, coincidentally, a slim volume about a painter (*Loutchansky,* 1932), much like the one that had begun his career nearly a quarter of a century before. After an excruciating, protracted illness (the effects of which were, however, never seen in his writing), Levinson died on December 3, 1933 at the age of 46. He had corrected the proofs of *Les Visages de la danse* on his deathbed and the volume appeared posthumously, as did his biography of Serge Lifar.

Many of Levinson's works have passed into oblivion, but he must nonetheless be considered the first real dance critic in France. (The task had previously been the domain of moonlighting theater and music critics.) He established a standard for dance criticism which has scarcely been equaled since. He had a unique gift of translating dance into words, and he was able to see not only "ballet's tinseled decor and exotic trappings, but the golden essence of the art."

Susan Cook Summer

Translator's Note

I N this translation, proper names and titles of productions are given in English transliteration, avoiding French and German renditions (Vroubel, *Schéhérazade*) wherever possible. Exceptions are naturally made in cases where names have already received a conventional form (Benois) which varies from the above guideline.

The notes found on the pages of the text itself are Levinson's, whereas those at the end of each chapter are mine.

Many people have offered assistance in the preparation of this work. I would like to express my thanks to Jill Silverman, who introduced me to Levinson and inspired this project. I would also like to thank Julia Brickell for her suggestions and encouragement, and Gerald Ackerman for his help with the picture research. I owe a special debt of gratitude to Richard Taruskin, who read the entire text, elucidated Levinson's stylistic eccentricities, and offered invaluable editorial comments.

Susan Cook Summer
New York, 1982

Author's Note

T H E S E pages do not presume to be, practically speaking, a treatise or the last word on the history of dance. I offer nothing more than a survey and analysis of gradually-accumulated theatrical impressions gathered together as a group of essays that are descriptive, theoretical and sometimes polemical in nature. These articles have appeared on the pages of both general and specialized journals and newspapers since 1911. Hoping to preserve an immediacy toward the subject, I have retained the original sequence and form of these spontaneous reactions as far as possible, only augmenting them with insertions and corrections prompted by my most recent experience. These systematic excerpts from my current critical work, embracing an important epoch of theatrical ferment, have formed the present summary of judgments about the "new and the old ballet."

The captivating and unparalleled revelation of classical dance provided the point of departure and the essence of my understanding of ballet, and lends a sense of unity to this account. I came out in "defense and glorification" of classical dance with my very first article. It so happened that my first contact with the classical tradition coincided with the beginnings of an energetic reaction against it. Thus in my defense of the traditional style I was obliged to take the opposite side and become a chronicler of the new departures in dance reform. I have in mind primarily the work of the ballet masters Fokine and Nijinsky as well as Isadora Duncan's remarkable achievements, for their endeavors have once again brought to the fore the most controversial issues in theatrical dance. In the realm of the visual arts, one may only believe one's own eyes: I have therefore extracted from a multitude of events and episodes only those which I was able to witness myself.

My first book on dance, *Masters of Ballet [Mastera baleta,* St. Petersburg, 1914], was primarily devoted to the history of attitudes toward the art. It set forth and interpreted, with the greatest possible fidelity, the aesthetic views of the more or less distant past. In a book about ballet "new and old," the author must face up to today's blazing artistic reality. This is no longer the place for the historian's impassive gaze. The justification for the theme I have chosen lies in my personal and confident approach to it and in my readiness to ardently uphold my own point of view. In order to provide a basis and material for discussion, my conclusions are preceded by a description of several productions.

André Levinson
February, 1917

Ballet Old and New

CHAPTER ONE

The New Ballet and the 'Saisons Russes' 1909-1911

T H E question of ballet—its historical vicissitudes and aesthetics, its past and its future—has reemerged only recently, and somewhat by chance. By chance because we, essentially recent disciples of the age-old tradition, came to the Russian ballet in a roundabout manner, via Paris and Berlin, and only looked back at "classical ballet" through all the novelties of Fokine, the ballet master-rebel and reformer.

The same confusion and arbitrary judgment that has reigned so long in the anarchical milieu of the dramatic theater can now be found in this new realm thanks to several circumstances: the predominating character of elemental Asiatic exoticism which the clamorous Parisian activity of Diaghilev has imparted to our art, the hostile suspicion of ballet as an art for the privileged and idle so deeply rooted in Russian intellectuals and men of letters, and, finally, the reversed historical perspective in which we, belated connoisseurs, have come to know the development of ballet forms.

Neophytes and zealots of the cult of Terpsichore that we are, only yesterday indifferent, perhaps, and strangers to the beautiful art of the dance, but deeply fascinated with it today, it ill behooves us to continue to talk about it in a sweeping, dogmatic manner, rigidly define its aesthetics, peremptorily point its path to the future. . . . But it is essential for us to know how to administer firmly and judiciously the priceless heritage that has been bequeathed to us.

Now that the gratifying rustle of European publicity that intoxicated so many has died down, now that the unprecedented brilliance of the Parisian premières no longer dazzles us, now that the dust of ignoble polemical clashes has settled, I would like to talk over our ballet with my readers.

Without prefacing these pages with premature generalizations, I would simply like to share some observations on the new phenomena that have inspired so many with love for the half-forgotten Muse of the Khorovod, left behind by her more intrepid sisters, and to consider some impressions and doubts with the readers.

My immediate goal is to describe the activities of Fokine and his associates in connection with the celebrated Parisian performances and to formulate those conclusions to which an attentive study of them has led me.

At the same time, the basic issues of theatrical dance will naturally be raised in the course of an all-round discussion of the art.

I
THE EASTERN SERIES:
CLEOPATRA, SHEHERAZADE

Cleopatra, one of Fokine's first productions, maintained for two whole "Saisons Russes" a position at the center of attention, at an invariable pinnacle of success.

The story of *Cleopatra*, vaguely reminiscent of Pushkin's *Egyptian Nights* and more concretely of Théophile Gautier's novella, *Une nuit de Cléopâtre*, develops against the background of a rather slight but elegant score by Arensky, and is magnificently framed by Bakst's decors. The St. Petersburg version of the ballet, more dignified though less opulent, remains faithful to Arensky's musical text whose motifs were drawn from the transcriptions of ethnographers and Egyptologists, and whose idea was apparently suggested by the famous dances from Saint-Saëns' *Samson and Delilah*. In Diaghilev's production, on the other hand, the original version was expanded and in parts replaced by a motley assortment of at times considerable fragments.

The action begins with a procession of temple servants bearing amphoras filled with water from the Nile. Ta-hor does not follow her friends; she is stopped by the appearance of Amoun, a young warrior. He has returned from the hunt. Ta-hor imitates the leaping and shyness of a chasing gazelle with youthful gaiety while Amoun pierces her with imaginary arrows, jokingly aimed from a taut bow. But all at once the hunter and his quarry are no more. Bellicose fervor gives way to amorous languor and a high priest who has arrived just in time blesses the union of the lovers who bow down before him in the rather intricate pose of Egyptian *orants*.

Suddenly the piercing, dissonant whistle of woodwinds (music from Rimsky-Korsakov's *Mlada*) bursts into the sacred silence of the temple and the morning, into the sweet violin melody. A brown slave in a white pinafore prostrates himself before the priest and announces the arrival of the Queen. Preceded by musicians carrying mysterious, ancient instruments, guards and a swarm of slave women, a long, closed case—a palanquin—is carried onto the stage. From behind the extended side of the palanquin, supported by the slaves' arms, the tall, immobile figure of a mummy in carved wooden buskins rises up. Circling about it, the slaves free it from its cerements which fall to the floor, one by one. When the last fetters have slipped away, the Queen comes down from the buskins. She is half nude, inhumanly tall and her hair is covered with blue powder. She moves toward a waiting couch and her movement bares a leg longer and better proportioned than those of the legendary figures of the Pre-Raphaelites. She is greeted with dances. But in Amoun's soul prayerful worship before the Queen's divine image gives way to another invincible, mad impulse. Plaintive Ta-hor vainly tries to hold him back. Pretending to have moved away, he places a love message on the tip of an arrow and shoots it at the Queen. Caught by the warriors, he mimes his burning, consuming desire. His desire will be heard, but at the price of his life. With an entreaty and the suasion of her chaste dance, small, dark Ta-hor makes a last vain

3

attempt to arouse the memory of bygone love games in the faithless one, and finally, in tears, she pleads with the regal lover, so merciless in her heartless voluptuousness. The contemptuous gesture with which the Queen returns the impertinent seeker of her love to his small, swarthy fiancée—despite the priest's mute reproach—decides Amoun's fate. A mobile curtain carried by slave women closes around the lovers and hides their amorous delights from the gaze of the uninitiated.

Meanwhile, the dances of the temple holiday continue. Temple servants and Cleopatra's slave women take their turns; the Hebrew captives' white-spotted brown cloaks flutter broadly.

The sacred ritual compels Ta-hor to perform the snake-charmer's dance before her triumphant rival. (In the original scenario, this *pas* of the *charmeuse de serpents*—apparently intended to be a separate "number"—was aptly assigned by the ballet master to Ta-hor, particularly as only she was able to perform the dance's coiling, overly flexible movements, suggestive and threatening, now accelerating to the mad spinning of a tarantella, now interrupted by acrobatic contortions.)

The bravura of a Bacchic round dance breaks into the ensuing pause (music from Glazunov's ballet *The Seasons;* the first rendition of the Autumn Bacchanale was Nikolai Legat's). Crowned with ivy, Bacchic couples take over the stage in a broad, willful run with knees thrust forward. They are half-dressed in ancient tunics and animal skins, their feet are bare. The crowd of bacchants rushes back along the sides clearing a passageway in which a single woman appears: the Mistress of the Feast. Bending her whole body forward, tossing back her head with a paralyzing gaze, parted lips and clenched teeth, flinging back her arms, throwing her bare knees up, she stamps the ground in a joyful frenzy. Paralyzed for an instant, the crowd again closes in around her. But into this stormy excitement an idyllic, pastoral note insinuates itself: mincing and skipping like a long-legged calf first let out to pasture, a young girl approaches the round dance. She is stealthily chased by two satyrs playing panpipes. The Mistress of the Dances notices the unexpected guest and draws her closer. Then, throwing back their torsos and linking arms, they both circle in place while the crowd of bacchants breaks up into separate circles and echoes their spinning movement. All of a sudden both satyrs, who had been awaiting a moment's fatigue from the dizzy dancing, throw themselves at the intended sacrifices, seize them and run away with their burdens followed by the enraged crowd.

Meanwhile, the queenly vampire is surfeited with love. The moment of retribution is at hand.

Repeating the very same gesture of battle and challenge, Ta-hor makes a last attempt to overcome Cleopatra's sinister will. She no longer fights for her own flouted love, but for the life of her beloved. But then the impassioned crowd of bacchants, temple servants, slaves and captives begins to flog her and, forcing her into the middle of the stage, they join hands and turn in an endless farandole. The unwinding snake of bodies coils around her in concentric circles. She tosses about in the center of the maelstrom and when, stunned and weak, she manages to tear herself out of the terrifying funnel, the disastrous act has already been committed. Faithless Amoun has paid for the Queen's caresses with fatal torture. Cleopatra takes delight in the sight of death, the motley flock of servant women, carried away by fear, takes wing and whirls away. Glutted with triumph, the Queen leaves the deserted sanctuary. Embracing the corpse of her beloved, Ta-hor bends down inconsolably.

Dance and action alternate in uninterrupted succession though, perhaps, the same dramatic theme of the unequal combat is too often repeated while the action, which develops to the accompaniment of melancholy melodies from Ancient Egypt, waves under the pressure of a new musical element in Glazunov's Bacchanale. Mussorgsky's Persian Dances (from the opera *Khovanshchina*) whose fairy tale polyphony contains—like fragrances in a crystal vessel— all the sensual charms of Persia, are brought into the finale of the ballet, disturbing with a contradiction the production's musical style and disrupting its scenic unity. Fokine was hardly right to deprive the Persian Dances of an interpretation unencumbered by a strange, alien subject.*

Bakst, who imparted a colorful animation to the severe forms of Egyptian art, without, however, keeping within the narrow confines of local color, harmed his work, in our view, by the application of an incongruous style. The figure of Cleopatra, seemingly a copy of one of Aubrey Beardsley's graphic apparitions, brings disharmony into the very heart of the ballet.

*When the opera *Khovanshchina* was produced at the Théâtre des Champs Elysées in 1913, these dances were staged by Adolph Bolm with decor by Fedorovsky.

And he drowns everything in an overabundance of diversity and richness of ethnographic and decorative material.

The symphonic suite *Sheherazade,* which served as a canvas for another of Fokine's choreographic fantasies, is one of the works in which Rimsky-Korsakov remains faithful to the element to which he owes his greatest achievements. A poem of the legendary East, "Sheherazade" is likewise a poem of the sea. To reach the shores of 1,001 nights, the composer placed his faith in the well-tried eye and fast ship of Sinbad the Sailor. Rimsky provided only laconic names for the individual sections of his work though his music, graphic *par excellence,* is sometimes almost onomatopoetic and easily lends itself to interpretation. The Sinbad motif, which is repeated throughout the entire work, is filled with foreboding energy and the decisiveness of battle. It is combined with a whole series of musical images of storm and calm, the waves' heavy pressure and rhythmic flow, the playful dance of white crests. And throughout this whole shifting panorama of the sea's elemental life, there twirls a delightful, capricious violin motif, decking the battle and Sinbad's shipwreck in bright, fairy tale garments.

The ballet's creators, Bakst and Fokine, were captivated by Rimsky's music, but could not interpret it precisely. They were forced to paraphrase his idea in their own way, developing the action of the prologue to *A Thousand and One Nights* against the background of Rimsky's tone poem. But this forced enterprise, though clever enough, was only partly successful.

The first movement of the symphony serves as the overture to the ballet.*

The curtain rises over a sumptuous scene of Eastern splendor. Before the spectator is the palace of the terrifying sovereign of India and China. Colossal drapes, green with gold and niello, give shade to the harem's retreat. To one side, under an enormous canopy, upon silken cushions and surrounded by his favorite wives in bright attire, reclines the all-powerful Shah Shariar. And nearby, strangely unmoving, lost in a mysterious dream, is the beautiful Sultana Zobeida. Sitting on a rug, their legs crossed in a typical Eastern pose, rocking back and forth with uplifted arms, three small, dark odalisques in wide orange pants delight the Sultan's gaze to the accompaniment of a light dance melody intoned by the bassoons and sup-

---

*The lyrical prelude from the third movement, *andantino quasi allegretto,* was eliminated from the score.

ported by the contrabasses. But then the odalisques rise up, move downstage with a rhythmic stride only to return again with a repeated movement. But the Shah, indifferent to the harmonious dance of the three orange peris, listens to the evil slander of his brother, Shah Zeman, and then the three odalisques, sliding in their slippers, silhouetted against the wall like a delightful reminder of the slippers worn by Beardsley's Salomé, disappear. The Shah commands trumpets to sound the hunt. The martial, brassy fanfare that announces his departure for the hunting grounds incites a feigned commotion among the wives who plead with their master not to abandon them. But servants rush in with armor for the Shah and his brother and, surrounded by warriors in deep blue caftans, turbans and burnooses, the Shah departs.

Before the trumpet calls have even stopped, the scene suddenly changes.

The wives circle around their incorruptible guard, the Chief Eunuch. And with gestures of entreaty and command, they whisper their secret desire. When he turns away, indifferent, they try to captivate him with the same light, alluring dance with which the odalisques tried to dispel the Shah's indomitable ennui. This reprise of the three soloists' motif by the whole crowd of dancers is one of the ballet master's most graceful inventions, though, of course, the ballet's purely choreographic content is practically exhausted by this one figure.

After a brief hesitation, the magnificent Eunuch, all dressed in purple and gold, yields to a bribe. He goes over to a bronze door at the back of the stage, unlocks it with an enormous key and in bursts a ferocious crowd of swarthy Hindus wearing bronze-colored clothes, wildly baring their teeth. Embraced by the Sultan's love-crazed concubines, their dark bodies fall onto the silken cushions. The Eunuch opens a second door, of silver, to let in Negroes in wide trousers of silver brocade. On mats in every corner, under the Shah's canopy, pairs of lovers twist in passionate ecstasy, coiling and tossing about. Meanwhile, reluctantly obeying the threatening command of Sultana Zobeida herself, the Eunuch opens a third door, of gold. After a moment of unbearable suspense, a pale gray mulatto throws himself into the embrace of his proud lover with a light jump. Wearing wide trousers of transparent gold cloth, the "beautiful beast of the race of tigers" is strong, seductive and has a childlike grin. The secret feast begins. Carrying dishes laden with fruit high above their heads, on the points of blue banners, a motley group of Hindu servant boys runs in with an elastic step on toe and circles the stage in a wide arc. Behind them follow, one after another in a continuous chain, green- and rose-colored almehs in dark veils. Soon the entire stage is enveloped in the whirlwind of a hugh round dance, interlacing in every conceivable figure like a coiling, heraldic snake. But suddenly the frenzied pace stops short in frozen horror. There is a pause on stage and in the orchestra. To the heavy beats of the Sinbad motif, the avenging Shah appears. The hunt was only a ruse whispered to Shariar by the wickedly clever Shah Zeman. Flight won't save the offenders; a savage horde of warriors overtakes them. Bloodied bodies lie about everywhere. A dead body even hangs over the canopy balustrade. Zobeida's lover—the mulatto—twirls like a top in mortal fear of death and falls, done to death by scimitars. Ten daggers are raised above the Sultana's head. Shariar lingers—in his mind he sees visions of bygone caresses. But with a gesture filled with mockery scornful Shah Zeman points to the body of the young mulatto. The irrepressible rage of the deceived Shah flares up and, breathless, Zobeida falls at his feet. And into this all too bloody orgy of slaughter and revenge there emerges—with an incongruity unforgivable in the ballet's creator—a wonderful, lyrical flute and oboe passage which Riemann, the German interpreter of Rimsky's symphony, shrewdly explained as an image of lightly curling clouds rising higher and higher over the now calm sea.

The production of *Sheherazade,* which called forth so many reprimands—mostly justified—in terms of musical treatment, was a triumph for Bakst, the designer, and his studies have been acquired by the Musée des Arts Décoratifs in Paris. But the decor designs, saturated with a brilliant, almost roaring multicolored effect of green, gold and orange shades (which could not have been more compatible with Rimsky-Korsakov's likewise purely decorative coloration), evoke another vision in the mind, a vision filled with potent and mysterious charms: "An Oriental Fairy Tale" by the immortal Vrubel. Completely analogous in construction, it is captivating with the harmonious colors of a Persian carpet, the ethereal aroma of perfumes from a gripping fairy tale secret, and the color language of a completely different order, like a holy night following a day full of cares. Bakst did not feel that there was anything more intimate than the depths of an Arabian fairy tale.

The choreographic suite *Les Orientales* in which the most diverse elements—a lackluster East and a dubious antiquity, Tcherepnine and Grieg—are carelessly combined, suffered a complete fiasco. This failure, which had no particular significance, concludes for now the series of Fokine and Bakst's remarkable Eastern fantasies.

II
THE ROMANTIC SERIES:
LE PAVILLON D'ARMIDE, CHOPINIANA, SCHUMANN'S *CARNAVAL*

I did not happen to see the Parisian version of *Le Pavillon d'Armide,* but the Russian public is quite familiar with the St. Petersburg production through its performances at the Maryinsky Theater, descriptions, reviews and exhibitions. Alexandre Benois' superlative scenario transports us from the turn of the eighteenth century to the era of Louis XIV, and from there to the Renaissance and the Age of Chivalry, as that era imagined it through its poets and musicians: Quinault, Lully and, later, Gluck.

Caught by a storm, a young traveler accepts the hospitality of an old-fashioned marquis, and has a dream in which the Gobelin tapestry hanging over the mantlepiece, "Rinaldo and Armida," comes to life with the marquis himself as a sorcerer. Armida bemoans Rinaldo's disappearance and the sleeper in his imagination identifies with Tasso's hero, Armida's lover. In a split reverie he sees himself confessing passionate love to his seductress and receiving her rose-colored scarf as a pledge of faithfulness. The dream vanishes and the morning, heralded by a shepherd's horn, brings not only awakening, but longing for the disappearing mirage and an irreparable split within his soul which teeters between the dream and reality. But when his trusty valet is finally able to tear his master away from pondering the again lifeless tapestry, the gracious marquis himself appears in a magnificent red caftan and leaning on a cane with a golden handle. He is a mixture of Voltaire and Dappertutto, of dream magician and genuine devil—but distinguished by the beautiful manners of the days of old. Seeing his guest to the door, the marquis hands him a forgotten item: Armida's rose-colored scarf which had been left on the mantlepiece. For an instant the dream and reality merge in the youth's mind. Jarred, his reason fails and he falls senseless into the valet's arms.

The story, whose very heart—the Gobelin tapestry coming to life—was taken from Théophile Gautier's novella *Omphale* (but is equally worthy of E. T. A. Hoffmann and coincides with his fantastic, artistic devices), received a very interesting pictorial treatment. The Gobelin hanging over the mantlepiece charmingly harks back to the ideas of Boucher and Le Moyne, the figures of the dream vision are "hours" in white camisoles, lanterns in hand, knights reminiscent of the Roi de Soleil in the *Ballet de la Nuit,* paradoxical magicians and wizards as well as veiled ladies summoned by their spells. All this is brought to life with colorful, stylish beauty. The pantomime is beautifully developed and in the finale reaches a climax of genuinely dramatic quality.

Tcherepnine's music, which was attractively orchestrated and quite sensitively adapted for dance, confines itself to only a few hints at eighteenth-century stylistic methods. And the dances themselves? Fokine replaces the measured, academic qualities of the old French *danse noble* with swift, complex movements—particularly in the ensembles—and with the nervous acceleration of tempo so characteristic of his style. Thus, not reflecting the style of the epoch to any degree whatsoever (which could have served as the artistic justification of the dances), the dances in *Armide* are reduced to a broken series of episodes and details drawn from the arsenal of classical dance. It is true that some of the poses and positions are captivating with their unusual play of foreshortening, their mechanical daring and complex symmetry, but all together the impression is feverish, disjointed, bustling and unstable. This *divertissement,* which the designer-librettist based completely on the period's distinctive style, on the verge of the grotesque, makes no impression whatsoever because of its total, formal lack of content. The only exception is the superlative dance of the clowns that combines a kicking dance and a jig.

The suite *Chopiniana* perhaps lies at the other extreme. It is the pure spirit of "classical" dance: on *pointe* and in tutus. These dances have a great deal of lyricism (even if it is a bit saccharine and foppish) in the opening nocturne, foaming passion in the mazurka, graceful and slightly affected pensiveness in the prelude. With a lightness completely out of the ordinary, a sylphide with little butterfly wings and a youth in a black camisole and light brown curls surrender to the rhythmic wave of the C-sharp minor waltz that carries them away. In the varied and ever poetic groupings of the *corps de ballet*, Fokine sensitively uses forms of the old dance theater—*Swan Lake* and *Giselle*—uniting them with a whole series of independent combinations. But this enticing "romantic daydream," as the ballet master called it, lacks one thing, perhaps: some sort of fantastic, lofty, amorous, slightly absurd fairy tale invention. These sylphides, ethereal and enigmatic, should have been spellbound princesses as in *Swan Lake* or wilis as in *Giselle*. Perhaps there is not enough pantomime, that "game of silence and guessing," as Paul Verlaine, the poet of poets, speaks of it, "which the music makes even more mute, where art even more faithfully conceals the secret it only whispers into the ear of Columbine or light-hearted Zulmé."[1]

In any event, the rare asset of this composition was the subordination of the ballet master's chance finds and passing whims to the imperative of a single style. And the poetic atmosphere of the idea was founded in this voluntary self-limitation. By constructing his ballet on the basis of a few simplified elements of classical technique, the ballet master made a significant improvement in its composition: the soloists' dance continually coordinates with the movements and ensembles of the *corps de ballet*. Nothing breaks up the unity of the image. There are no onlookers or outsiders on stage; no one departs from the action or beat even for an instant. This is an unquestionable improvement in comparison to the usual deployment of a ballet stage where an exacting spectator is perpetually required to close his eyes to the presence of undisciplined masses not participating in the action. The groups of "sylphides" are reminiscent of many good examples; the *enchaînements* and transitions from one grouping to the next are inventive and attractive.

Meanwhile, another obstacle to that *illusion dans le décor* that Verlaine seeks, is the presumptuous venture to orchestrate Chopin—a venture that defeated even those masters of the orchestra who performed the task for the Parisian production. But this brings us to the basic question of interpreting music through dance—a question to which we will turn later.

The ballet master set himself just such a task of choreographically interpreting a musical idea in Schumann's *Carnaval*. In the episodes of *Carnaval*, in the brilliant *scènes mignonnes*, Schumann's divided self is shown in all possible nuances: the proud spirit of headlong, impetuous Schumann-Florestan and the heart of Schumann-Eusebius, exhausted from a surfeit of sweet melancholy.

The curtain rises to reveal a completely empty stage draped in green "cloths" which cover the back and hide the wings. The only prop is a couch at the rear. Slipping in and out of the folds in the drapery, appearing and disappearing, chasing each other are women in black masks and men in tall top hats. Languid Chiarina—all the comfort and promise of caresses, beckoning and elusive; passionate Estrella with sudden moments of reflection; irrepressible Florestan, bursting with spontaneous enthusiasm; Eusebius, sighing vainly as all rush by and, finally, lagging behind, farinaceous Pierrot, dressed as the carnival Fortune. Huge, ridiculous and good humored, he dashes about only to fall over the prompter's box. A mischievous pair—motley Harlequin and Columbine in lace—try to hide their amorous entente from an immodest dandy in green gloves, the persistent Pantalon. Flitting across the stage with a flying leap is a spirited butterfly, Papillon. And when the figure of Chopin floats over the orchestra to a gentle cantilena, three masked fairies appear from behind the thick drapes, rise on toe, join hands and are suddenly rigid and silent, as if confiding some kind of mournful secret to each other. But then the stage is filled with the rustling of white skirts and restrained smiles beneath half masks and, to the strains of a *valse noble,* we are captivated by the rhythmic circling of couples and the light patter of quick little feet.

Then the playful carnival crowd unites, circles around the gentle, lighthearted love of Harlequin and Columbine and whirls away in a final dance—to the bold strains of the Davidsbündler march—twirling and stunning the cowering, indignant crowd of Philistines in red top hats with their pompous wives. The curtain falls: Pierrot and Pantalon fail to jump back in time and are caught in a ridiculous position between the footlights and the curtain—an amusing trick, but one I saw long ago somewhere in a music hall.

As far as I know, the ballet's first production was back in St. Petersburg amidst the sounds and sparkle of a Shrovetide masquerade in a hall where hundreds of dancers were already whirling, dashing about and enjoying themselves. The harlequinade on stage took place against the background of the masquerade in the hall. This circumstance, perhaps, concealed the visual skimpiness so evident in the production *à grand spectacle.*

Schumann's prelude, all by itself, is already an impetuous call to

carnival revelry, the festive animation of the hurrying crowd, eager
for the illusory pleasures of the wild holiday (to say nothing of the
uncontrolled, mad dash of the final galop)—the prelude already creates an atmosphere of a motley, endless human stream from whose
violent waves one can distinguish the fleeting images of Schumann's fantasy, images which are then swallowed up once again.
But this mood instantly crumbles at the sight of the stage's "Torri-
cellian vacuum" and the sober, meager draperies. What is the good
of all the pranks played by Harlequin-the-top, all Pierrot's ridiculous bewilderment, all Papillon's fluttering about when there is no
occasion for it and the main thing, namely, the carnival, is missing?
Bakst's wonderful costumes are in keeping with the Philistine-
Romantic Biedermeier style, but can this style, so neat and intimate,
be identified with the images of Schumann's visual imagination,
images that are hardly mere puppets? The genre, so successfully
used by Karl Walser in a revival of an old Viennese comedy at Max
Reinhardt's Deutsches Theater, and by Bakst himself in *Die Puppenfee,* might correspond to but one episode of the Schumann carnival, the *valse allemande.* And what became of those treasures of shy
tenderness that were hidden beneath the light irony and piquant
grace, under the humorous dialogue of *reconnaissance?* Fokine's
production contains a marvelous detail: Harlequin, kneeling before
Columbine, pulls the red heart of a mechanical doll out from his
checked shirt as a token of eternal love and places it at the feet of his
beloved.

But the wooden heart of Schumann's doll can shed real blood.

And this is why it somehow seems to me that Fokine's sweet toys
do not reach the plane of Schumann's inspiration. They whirl
around, slip away and disappear.

III
THE NATIONAL SERIES:
FESTIN, FIREBIRD

The choreographic suite *Le Festin* is almost completely outside the
realm of Fokine's work, which is represented only by the Lezghinka
from *The Demon.* The rest consists of the mazurka from *Swan Lake,*
Petipa's "Blue Bird," renamed "Gold" because of the new costumes[2] (from *The Sleeping Beauty*), and a classical *pas de deux.*

Only the production of the ballet-fairy tale *Firebird,* choreographed to the music of Igor Stravinsky, revealed to Fokine a wide scope of creative possibilities within the realm of Russian national subjects.

The Russian public did not react favorably to this music when it was performed at a symphonic concert conducted by Ziloti. Despite its unusual sparkle and varied orchestration, despite the novelty of many harmonic combinations—which are fully appreciated only by the specialists—the work of this talented pupil of Rimsky-Korsakov is marked by an extreme poverty of melodic invention. It is a complex, colorful mosaic of sounds completely lacking in the epic, long breathed character that distinguishes Rimsky's fairy tale works.

It is twilight on stage; here and there Golovin's decor shines deep gold. Accompanied by the heavy throb of basses in the orchestra, there appears an enormous horseman on a firmly-stepping black steed—it is the Night. Morning begins to break: in the hazy distance the indistinct outlines of Eastern architecture—Kashchei's castle—become visible while in the foreground, in the sorcerer's garden, surrounded by a stone wall, golden apples sparkle on the forbidden tree. But then, sharp tongues of flame seem to spring up from the orchestra like the delicate crackle and hiss of an unseen fire and, flying high above the garden the Firebird appears in bright plumage of green, red and gold. She lands near the tree with the golden apples and, fluttering about, fails to notice Ivan Tsarevich who has climbed the wall and is following her. He manages to catch the wondrous bird. She wants to break loose, fly off, but his strong hand holds her fast. Whether it was a difficulty with the musical rhythm or the technical inadequacy of the *danseuse,* the impression created was just the opposite, and was annoyingly silly. It looked as though Ivan Tsarevich were attempting in vain to hoist the Firebird into the air, to force her to leave the ground and fly while she, meanwhile, was foiling his plan. She begs the Tsarevich to return her freedom, promising to help him at a time of need and, though the violins did not echo her entreaty very expressively, the Tsarevich gives in and grants her freedom, first plucking a few feathers from her multicolored raiment. The Firebird hastens away, but a new, captivating sight awaits the Tsarevich who lurks behind the bushes. A crowd of princesses taken captive by Kashchei descends from a high tower. In long chemises of white linen with colorful embroidery, they skip around the tree and toss and catch the golden apples. Ivan abandons his hiding place and, not without difficulty, overtakes the fleet-footed girls. They hide behind the eldest, like chicks from a vulture, and she raises her arms in defense while the long file of princesses, scurrying about in every direction, sweeps the ground like a long, white fluffy tail. But Ivan Tsarevich's chestnut curls and dashing bravery claim their own, and the first princess confides in the visitor and relates the sad tale of her abduction. Ivan's stout heart is set aflame. . . . In all their games and engaging conversation the girls have not noticed that the dawn clouds have given way to a radiant morning, and only when a white horseman—the Day on a silver steed—passes by the enchanted garden do they rouse themselves and disappear, obedient to their all-powerful spell.

Ivan thinks of running away, but an unprecedented sight roots him to the spot. From on high, down from the fantastic galleries, preceded by the terrible green faces of werewolves, surrounded by guards, grey sorcerers, young maidens attired in red, amidst a devilish whistle and din, deathless Kashchei himself, enormous, his beard reaching to the ground, his fingers like tree trunks, descends into the forbidden garden. Leaning on his staff, supported under the arms by servants, he slowly moves toward Ivan, who stands frozen in terror. The Tsarevich wants to tear away, scale the wall. He tries to run but fearsome warriors in tall, Persian hats and gold brocade caftans with lilac lapels catch up to him first, pin him to the ground and threaten him with short scimitars. Kashchei's rage flares up with a vengeance at the uninvited guest who dared to breach the forbidden garden, and he threatens the Tsarevich with the fate of many a bold hero: to be turned into stone with a wave of Kashchei's hand. But in the midst of this terrible calamity, Ivan remembers the three feathers from the Firebird. She comes flying in obedient response to his call, circles among the dumbfounded crowd of sorcerers and ensnares them with unexpected charms while in the orchestra there reappears, glittering and sparkling, the golden "Magic Fire" motif. She dances and catches everyone up in her dance: the warriors and maidens, the green monsters, even Kashchei himself. Her spells are irresistible. By this time the evil powers cannot stop their dance, they are powerless to slow down its furious pace. And the sorcerers rush ever faster in the "infernal dance," stamping frenziedly in place, whirling in a khorovod. But then the whole accumulated forte in the orchestra breaks off and, accompanied by the quiet crackle of woodwinds, the dance continues in the terrible, suffocating silence until the brass fanfare strikes up again, and the mad crowd stamps, races and spins faster and faster. . . . Suddenly an enormous white egg appears in the arms of Ivan Tsarevich. He waves it at Kashchei who recoils in mortal terror while continuing to stamp in place all the while. Ivan throws it and, when it breaks, Kashchei falls lifeless. In an instant the evil spells are broken, the fiends of the night hide and the triumphant Ivan frees the enchanted princesses and accepts the thanks of the transformed heroes who appear from the stone wall as it suddenly springs to life. They all acclaim Ivan and the princess offers him her hand; the golden apples of Kashchei's garden will be her dowry.

Golovin's decors were of a wondrous, fairy tale style—almost like gingerbread—of brown and green with gold, though they had an obvious Eastern motif. The costumes had a fantastic Oriental style and coloration, though perhaps somewhat subdued in comparison with Bakst.[3] Only the captive princesses' white chemises, which so vividly recall Polenova's paintings, and Ivan Tsarevich's caftan and hat have a purely Russian flavor—a flavor so weakly expressed in the music. In the one Russian dance from *The Little Humpbacked Horse* that was included in *Le Festin* and apparently choreographed by the late Grantseva, there is more local color than in the entire *Firebird*—there is more Russian fluidity, laziness and sudden animation.

Golovin's splendid production can justifiably be placed alongside Bakst's Oriental fantasies, but to regard *Firebird* as a contribution to the national mythology would be frivolous to say the least. It has nothing in common with real folk art and even the plot of the folk tale was presented in the scenario in an insipid, confused way. In the dances themselves there is almost no use of folk motifs. And there are no such dances at all, by the way, in Fokine's latest production either, but we will come to that later. In addition, we must bear in mind that this production, according to those close to Russian art in Paris, had a hasty, unfinished quality and did not completely accord with the authors' original intentions. It is hard for us to take into account this element of chance.

It is only clear that Kashchei's forbidden garden, as seen in *Firebird,* could, on the basis of its visual embodiment, could amost as well have been called the "Garden of Hesperides."

IV
THE "SAISON RUSSE" AT THE GRAND OPÉRA:
NARCISSE, LE SPECTRE DE LA ROSE,
SADKO, PETRUSHKA

The 1911 "Saison Russe," transplanted onto the Opéra's "official" stage (earlier engagements took place at the Châtelet Theater, a private stage equipped for fantastic productions in folk style), was marked by new efforts on the part of Russian modernistic ballet to consolidate its position established during recent years as first in the world—efforts no less interesting than their predecessors. The intentions of Serge Diaghilev, the initiator of the "Saisons," were, as before, realized by a phalanx of celebrated associates: the composers Igor Stravinsky and Tcherepnine, the ballet master Fokine, the painters Bakst, Anisfeld and Alexandre Benois, who is the artistic arbiter of the whole enterprise. Only the company of performers was different, lacking many of the most "representative" participants in the Russian ballet.

Alongside revivals of *Sheherazade* and *Carnaval* (enriched by new drapery), the season's new attractions were *Narcisse* by Bakst and Tcherepnine, the underwater kingdom from *Sadko* by Rimsky-Korsakov (preserving the vocal parts and choruses), *Le Spectre de la Rose* by Bakst and *Petrushka* by Stravinsky and Benois.

The subject of *Narcisse,* Bakst's tragic idyll, has more than once been the object of choreographic treatment. The famous Carlo Blasis staged the anacreotonic ballet *La Ninfa Eco* at the Teatro Municipale in Piacenza about seventy years ago. In our day, Isadora Duncan touched upon the same subject, if only episodically. Here is how the latest interpreters have adapted the ancient idea.

Amid dark cliffs shaded by flowing emerald foliage, next to a too obviously artificial stream, small green spirits awaken and greet the morning with the primitive dance-games of amphibious deities. They crawl onto each others' backs, roll on the ground and hide the instant they see couples pouring into the garden. They seek out shade. Out in the cloudy meadows visible through rocky gates (a two-tiered structure reminiscent of Torelli and productions of the *Grand siècle*) a heavy, blue sultriness already hangs in the air. Young men and maidens wearing light tunics, the traditional residents of cheerful "terra cotta" Greece with its gay and somewhat sweet colors (green with pale blue under the sky and trees; brick and lemon colors on their clothes), circle around a young girl in a solemn, sacramental procession. She performs a half-"comic," half-Bacchic dance. A bacchante bursts in upon this archaeologically and choreographically dual movement, throwing her head and torso back into the arms of the friends accompanying her and, standing up straight, imparts the accelerated tempo and frenzied circling of a bacchanale into the sluggish crowd.

Distant voices are heard from beyond the cliffs; the song of Narcissus and the tearful voice of the nymph Echo, spellbound by Pan, involuntarily mimicking the handsome shepherd.

The girls surround Narcissus who has run up, rose-colored and wearing a white, sleeveless tunic. They are captivated by the ephebe's beauty, the powerful strength of his physique, his childlike smile and the feminine, ingratiating quality of his affected gestures. Narcissus is not completely indifferent to the tempestuous waves of passionate desire, to the thrill of an unexpected touch. In his innocent naiveté he is perplexed, for he has not yet grasped the secret of his beauty which causes the hearts of maidens to throb. Slipping out from behind a cliff, spellbound Echo follows Narcissus. She is grief itself, robed in hyacinth garments, more mournful than black. And she bows down before the indifferent one with a hopeless entreaty of unrequited passion. He responds insouciantly to her caresses. But, stung with jealousy, the foolish rival nymphs divulge to Narcissus the secret of Echo's curse. And indeed, the nymph answers each of Narcissus' movements by repeating it. The strange game beguiles the shepherd and, with childlike cruelty, he mocks Echo's sufferings and runs off, finally, lured by the derisive chorus. Raising her hands in prayer, the wounded nymph calls for the anger of the gods to fall on the impertinent one. Narcissus returns, tormented by thirst, and bends over the stream where he freezes at the sight of his own beauty. He only tears his face from the mirror-like surface so that rising, his body is reflected in countless movements and poses. Terrified at her own curse, Echo tries in vain to deflect his gaze, to distract his thought. He pushes her aside and once again becomes absorbed in contemplating his own beauty. He leans lower and lower over the stream and, finally, disappears into its waters. The alarmed spirits, all the green creatures of the bright depths, leave their burrows to mourn for Narcissus while horror and contrition turn the guilty nymph into stone. And, from the depths that have claimed Narcissus, there rises majestically an enormous white flower.

In Bakst and Fokine's scenic interpretation of this Ovidian metamorphosis, the usual repertoire of ancient movements is somewhat enriched in comparison to Isadora Duncan's school, that of *Eunice* and in the Bacchanale. In particular, the performer who danced the part of Echo succeeded in combining some traditional gestures of Greek funeral pantomime with the psychological demands of her role. The Echo myth dresses an *acoustical* phenomenon in an anthropomorphic form. The ballet master succeeded in translating it most cleverly into *mimetic* language, though he found it necessary to preserve the subject's original setting. With this in mind, he introduced a *vocal* element. It is true that as authoritative a ballet theoretician as Noverre allows the introduction of a chorus singing offstage to intensify the feeling of horror (the "Danaides" program), but in the present instance the technique only assists the utter corruption of ballet form. (A similar device was already used in *The Nutcracker* by Tchaikovsky and Lev Ivanov, but there the chorus played a purely musical, and by no means active, role.)

The choreographic miniature, *Le Spectre de la Rose,* combines, by for the most part a happy whim, Weber's music as orchestrated by Berlioz *(Invitation to the Dance)* with the subject of a poem by Théophile Gautier. Returning from a ball, a young girl in a white calf-length dress with a flounce and a *povoynik* with wide ribbons (as in the drawings of Achille Dervéria) falls asleep in an armchair, breathing in the aroma of a rose. In her dream, prompted by the memories of the last turn, there appears the spirit of the rose plucked for her: a handsome youth dressed in the faded violet petals of the dying flower. He circles around her in a somnambulant waltz on toe and disappears into the mist while she bends in sleepy languor over the arm of the chair. The intimate romance of this "chamber" scene does not completely harmonize with the production *à grand spectacle* or the decor in blue and white tones which Bakst involuntarily imbued with the usual intense coloration of his decorative style.

In the season's third novelty, an act from *Sadko,* the ballet master did not (as he did in *Sheherazade*) force a foreign dramatic content onto Rimsky-Korsakov's score. Here he appeared as the legitimate interpreter of the composer's intentions. I am only not sure that the content of the ballet-divertissement that illustrates this act is worthy of being singled out as an independent "opus." Just as Stravinsky's prematurely faded *Firebird* (fated, perhaps, to rise again to a longer life on the concert stage) has its Bird-Maiden spell, so in *Sadko* the Novgorodian guest playing his *gusli* is a signal for building up a general dance in a gradually accelerating tempo. Similar in construction to Stravinsky's work, *Sadko* is just as poor in dances, if you do not count the inevitable *khorovods*. Fokine, however, created a whole series of new groupings for *Sadko,* somewhat abusing his standard technique of placing the dancers on the ground in a recumbent position. The choreographic side creates a rather disappointing impression as, in keeping with the subject's demands, it is thrust onto one of the singing performers and onto the clumsy, though well disciplined chorus. Anisfeld's artistic imagination follows right in the footsteps of Golovin and, particularly, Bakst, with a considerable inclination toward prettiness.

But the real artistic victory that saved Diaghilev's enterprise from the inevitable accusation of monotony was *Petrushka* by Stravinsky and Benois. This was first of all a victory for the composer, whose powerful mastery wove the most unexpected and suggestive harmonies from the dissonant, turbulent rumble of a folk carnival, from the whoop and stamping of an exuberant dance, from the noisy jingles of an old farceur, from the jumbled clamor, clatter and clang of the streaming crowd, the tinkle of little bells on the jester's cap, the rapping of wooden rattles—a chaos of sounds into which there pours, barely ringing and wheezing, the babbling of a dilapidated barrel organ sometimes drowned out by the drunken roar of an accordion and the, by contrast, almost eerie, needle-like sharpness and clarity of the tinny flute solo with which a mysterious Oriental summons his audience. He is a magician and a wizard in a yellow robe and a high hat. His magical pipe gradually forces the holiday commotion to subside. The tiresome "old man" falls silent, the street dancer rolls up her trampled rug, and the curtains of a fairground booth slide apart to reveal three dolls: a black-skinned Moor in a green caftan all sewn up in lace; a Ballerina doll in a short lilac skirt revealing red bloomers that match her bodice (trimmed with a fringe of pillow lace) and shod in traditional ballet slippers; and finally Petrushka himself with his tassled cap. In time to the music the dolls dither on their iron posts until the host's magic wand permits them to step forward and continue their mechanical dance amid the dumbfounded gapers. The Moor tries to embrace the Ballerina, but in Petrushka's hands there appears a truncheon—the legacy of his Italian cousin Arlecchino—and he beats the enterprising Moor about the neck. The Moor chases him with a scimitar and in the midst of the merriment, Petrushka flees to safety. The curtain falls for an instant and rises again to reveal the interior of the fair booth. All alone, though under the ever watchful eye of the magician whose portrait stands out on the black backdrop, Petrushka, with a gesture of despair, mimes the hidden sufferings of his soul repressed within his clown-like puppet's body: his jealous and bashful love for the Ballerina. She suddenly appears in the doorway but, instead of a passionate confession, Petrushka's doll body twists in a comical, ungainly convulsion. She recoils in contempt and disgust. Meanwhile, the Moor ignores the situation and takes a well-deserved rest amidst the carpets and pillows of his Eastern tent in which Persia's colorful, ornamental luxury was translated into the hyperbolic language of a *lubok* for some odd reason. He tries to crack the shell of a coconut and, turning it on all sides, blunting his scimitar on it, he prostrates himself before the stubborn nut as if before a diety. A brass trumpet in her hands, the Ballerina slips into the tent and dances on *pointe* with the sonorous instrument placed at her lips. The Moor has forgotten all about the puzzling nut when a desperate Petrushka unexpectedly interrupts his amusements—but Petrushka has to flee from the scimitar. The Ballerina's fear of Petrushka's unbidden jealousy gives her an excuse to seek protection in the strong embraces of her swarthy deliverer.

Meanwhile, outside, the square swirls in holiday intoxication: beauteous "nursemaids" in *sarafans* and *kokoshniks* stream by, spreading their arms and waving their hands; coachmen in colorful *poddyovkas* with lace on their hats click their heels with spirit; boisterous young lads leap into a *prisiadka*; mummers wearing dreadful masks mix into the crowd while elegant ladies accompanied by stately officers in three-cornered hats and greatcoats and by dandies in overcoats fastidiously observe the crude amusements of the common folk through their lorgnettes.

Suddenly, the booth curtains slide apart and out runs Petrushka, followed by the victorious Moor. The scimitar flashes and Petrushka collapses to the ground lifeless, cut in two. Aghast at the verisimilitude of the spectacle, the crowd calls to a police officer for help, they drag the dolls' master through the gates and he, laughing, shows the crowd the wooden halves of Petrushka's head. The people disperse and, regaining his composure, the magician drags the pieces of the unlucky doll into his tent. But all of a sudden he stops, struck by the appearance of Petrushka's double on the balustrade of the booth, and he flees in terror. Separated from its body, Petrushka's living soul mourns the death of its earthly cover.

Here we see that in this new production, Benois the designer, costumer and historian of Russian life during the 1830s (which he described with such loving irony, lightly adorned with Western Romanticism) and Benois the visionary of form and color have left Benois the librettist way behind. The behind-the-scenes psychology of the dolls, in whose veins "cranberry juice" mixes with real blood, has already been overused in the ballets *Die Puppenfee, The Nutcracker,* Offenbach's famous opera *[Les Contes d'Hoffmann]* and, particularly, *Coppélia.*

This more or less sums up the contents of the Russian ballet performances in Paris as well as Fokine's achievement as a ballet master. Some productions of his, which have not been mentioned here, will be touched upon later in my exposition.

As far as possible I have presented the stories of the ballets, revealed their choreographic content, described their staging and discussed their relationship to the accompanying music. But my evaluations have not gone beyond personal remarks or a critique of individual aspects of Fokine's conceptions. I shall now move on to some generalizations and shall attempt to characterize the fundamental principles of Fokine's reforming work as well as to evaluate its results by comparing them to the forms of traditional, "classical" ballet.

Perhaps this path will lead us away from cursory and curious comments to specific, sober judgments. Our next task is to search for the origin, the starting point of Fokine's choreographic quest. The primary source seems to be his infatuation with antiquity by way of Isadora Duncan's art.

Notes to Chapter One

1. See: *Oeuvres Complètes de Paul Verlaine,* Volume III (Paris: Albert Messein, 1927), pp. 220–221.
2. The Blue Bird *pas de deux* from Marius Petipa's ballet *The Sleeping Beauty* was presented in *Le Festin* with Tamara Karsavina in a brilliant orange and gold

costume. The *pas de deux* has been variously called "L'Oiseau de feu," "L'Oiseau d'or," "L'Oiseau et le prince."

3. In this production, Bakst designed the costumes for the principal dancers while the rest of the costumes and the decor were designed by Golovin.

CHAPTER TWO

The Art and Meaning of Isadora Duncan

S I N C E our ballet theater has been until recently the exclusive property of a small circle and has been shunned by the general public on account of prejudices that have still not been completely overcome, the individual form through which the art of the dance came really close to us, disturbing us deeply and fruitfully, was the dance of Isadora Duncan.

The courageous artist did not immediately win our sympathy, but her wide recognition (which coincided with a certain decline in her style) elicited evaluations as enthusiastic as they were superficial.

Having instinctively given credit to the new beauty revealed by Miss Duncan, friends of her art in the public and the press went on to create a completely fictitious and inappropriate criterion for evaluating her dance: they identified it with ancient dance.

We know relatively little about ancient dance; its living tradition has been irretrievably lost. Mainly we know about its profound link with cult worship. Acknowledging the absence of a religious basis in her endeavors, Miss Duncan herself wisely denies that her art is a direct, organic perpetuation of antiquity. Her dance, she affirms in her public lecture, is not a dance of the past but a dance of the future. But if in her art there is no genuine link with the little-known essence of ancient dance, then her ideological, I would say even moral, basis coincides with the somewhat simplified and vulgarized Hellenism of our day, whose slogans are: freedom of the body, the cult of sculptural, tactile beauty—a cult nourished by beautiful museum recollections.

We see no need to confuse this Hellenism of ours with the difficult-to-comprehend, organic character of ancient culture.

Fanatics of Duncan's art, hoping to find a measure of support for their reasoning, and to justify their enthusiasm in the eyes of skeptics, greatly overestimate the importance of such museum recollections.

There is no question that Miss Duncan's assiduous study of ancient sculpture, relief and especially vase painting (all of which have developed and enriched her dance) was a serious and meritorious endeavor. But it would be deeply erroneous to see this as her innovation or the ''gospel'' of her art.

The fact is that the use of ancient prototypes as creative material and the reconstruction of antiquity according to extant artistic documents have made it possible to renew the traditions of both choreography and the dramatic stage.

It is possible that many have failed to discern through the fascinating veil of creative individualism that the unparalleled evocation of antiquity is one of the main attractions of Sarah Bernhardt's interpretation of Racine's *Phèdre*. It is no accident that the *création* of this image (as the French say) was preceded by an extensive study of museum treasures, even including the Attic vases of our own Hermitage.

The basic inability of the plastic arts, sculpture and painting, to reproduce movement in all its consecutive moments has been the fatal obstacle to attempts at restoring ancient dance forms.

These art forms can only fix a single instant of a movement, chiefly its beginning or end. Sculpture is especially static as it is bound by the laws of equilibrium.

For this reason ancient art has only been able to preserve for us a series of poses and positions. It is not within its powers to give us a complete conception of the dynamics of dance or of movement itself.

Even the most dignified and resourceful attempts to reconstruct ancient dance inevitably bear the mark of incompleteness and caprice.

But Duncan's art, though not tied genetically to antiquity, is all the more indebted to the slogans of contemporary Hellenism: that the body be freed from clothing, the cult of corporeality reborn. The ideal of complete nudity in dance—which Duncan did not achieve only because of police interference—hardly coincides with ancient aesthetics which fully appreciated the choreographic significance of clothing and drapery. Consequently, these slogans cannot be assigned to the realm of *purely aesthetic* thought. They overly emphasize the ethical aspect of protest against false shame, against hermetically-sealed philistinism—in a word, they represent a somewhat naive invective against a conventional lie.

Another issue, immeasurably richer in its social implications, is the purely hygienic concern about the physical development of the younger generation and the struggle with approaching degeneracy.

Duncan's innovation in the area of dance naturally complements the blossoming of different types of sport and the formation of all sorts of gymnastic organizations that we have witnessed during the past decade. In choreography, Duncan's dance was similar to the effect of the natural corset or the dress of reform in the world of fashion.

And it is quite natural that Isadora Duncan sought not so much to create a new phalanx of refined artists as to address the pedagogical goal of generally disseminating her endeavors among the masses. It is not without reason that A[rkady] G[eorgievich] Gornfel'd in his "little eulogy" to the artist, interpreted the meaning of her art as "the possibility for all of us to be beautiful" *(Books and People)*.[2]

Not only the influence of modern times, but also Duncan's *racial* qualities affected this cult of athleticism, of the strong, lithe, satisfied and healthy body. The aesthetic nature of her dance has that typically *Anglo-Saxon* mark. This characteristic is best described by a term already in use for another aspect of English artistic culture: "Pre-Raphaelitism."

Pre-Raphaelitism is that reactionary movement which brings over-refined classical and post-classical forms back to the level of primitive conceptions. It is a compromise movement, not strong enough to break decisively with academic traditions, and therefore it did not return to the initial stage of development, but timidly stopped short on the latest possible step. English Pre-Raphaelite artists broke with the powerful maturity of the cinquecento in favor of Botticelli and Verrocchio; none of them approached Giotto.

Duncan has that vividness of form, that absence of chiaroscuro, that concreteness of style that characterizes quattrocento painting. In her *Ange avec violon,* in her poetic *Primavera* there is all the healthy strength of the good Lorenzo di Credi, softened by Botticelli's fragile intellectualism. Duncan has that romantic yet not overly profound *nostalgie du passé* that appeared in the treatment of antiquity during the quattrocento. She has that idyllic note, that inability to capture the monumental and hieratic such as we see in the work of a Pietro di Cosimo, whose Venus reposes amidst the multicolored flowers of a Tuscan glade while a butterfly momentarily alights on her bared knee.

In essence Duncan's dance is *mimed,* figurative. It draws its forms from imitations of natural, ordinary poses and movements and from the direct mimed portrayal of emotional experiences. And this constitutes not her identity with, but her deep *analogical* similarity to ancient *orcheisthai.*

In *Ange avec violon* she imitates an arm bowing a real violin; in *Primavera,* a graphic copy of Botticelli's painting, countless flowers strewn by Spring fall from her half-closed fingers; in Grechaninov's *Lullaby* she seems to bend over the infant's cradle and, when her Narcissus bends his beautiful knee over the imaginary stream into which he gazes, the audience can feel the moisture and transparency of the current, and the shiver of sudden coldness going through his body. As in Goethe's ballad,[3] moisture scooped up by the Brahmin's wife turns into a crystal ball, so Duncan's mimetic gesture scoops up imaginary objects from the surrounding atmosphere, revitalizing them with concrete, tactile life. And that is why her use of certain props—palm branches, golden leaves in Tchaikovsky's *Romance*—seems to be a certain lapse in her style, an unnecessary infringement on her original purity.

She extracts the mimetic, let us say even *dramatic* content of her dance from her impressions of the accompanying music. The nature of her musical sensibility, which has aroused so much comment as to whether she "*correctly* dances Chopin, Grieg, Beethoven," and even a whole musicians' crusade is not in the end susceptible to verification. The images and moods created in our consciousness by irrational forces cannot be identical for everybody, and therefore cannot be made binding for everybody.

The extent to which music can inspire moods and movements was brought home to me by the extraordinary example of somnambulist Madeleine dancing under hypnosis. Her will is paralyzed and the only source of her dance is the musical rhythm, that irresistible command acting directly upon her imagination and replacing the will. From this arises the diversity of her dance and the sometimes frenzied access of dramatic passion.

In depicting spiritual moods, Duncan does not exceed the limits of realistic movement. Freed from the constraints of clothing, her dance is a wide, willful run. Her dance is not characterized by jumps—one of the primary elements of classical ballet—or by movement on toe which subordinates the ballerina's whole body— her head, her arms—to the laws of a special equilibrium. Duncan's head is freely thrust back or bent forward, her hands—independent of the general movement of the arms—live an expressive life of their own. And in this there is yet another analogy to ancient dance. While her head, arms and torso rock right and left at the beginning of a Strauss waltz, passively, indecisively, as if lulled by the rhythm—an impatient foot simply taps out the beat.

Impressions from Duncan's last visit allowed these separate comments to coalesce into something more concrete and definite. Here she took on such challenges to the art of plastic and dramatic embodiment as Gluck's *Orfeo* and Richard Wagner's *Wesendonk Lieder*.

After the orchestral overture, a mournful Orpheus emerges from a dark corner of the stage draped with cloth and unevenly lit with violet. His head is tilted back, his arms hang at his sides. In this long, funereal state his mood is revealed only by his agonizingly slow pace. His overly long garments, which seem to drag his body back and impede his movements, fall in straight, severe pleats. It is this material constraint that informs Duncan's movements with a sense of impotent despair until she extends a conjuring arm upward with fingers outstretched. Then, as a violin intones Orpheus' repeated cry, "Eurydice! Eurydice!" she bends over an imaginary grave and with gestures of utmost tenderness breaks the solemn, severe ritual of sepulchral ceremony. This action, executed by Duncan with extreme economy of figurative means, lacks virtually all trace of ancient funeral mime. Ancient mourners invariably simulated the pulling out of their hair by placing a crooked arm over their heads. Here Duncan's performance is based not on archaeology but on actual feeling. It's true that this feeling is not terribly deep, but such grandeur of conception is outside the dancer's scope.

The second scene—the chorus and dances of the Furies, later to be spellbound by Orpheus' lyre—was less attractively conceived. It is true that Duncan skillfully manages to evoke the impression of an antic chorus of multitudes. She is able to convey the orchestra's alarming dissonances by the sudden breaks in the sculptural line. But the dance itself fails because of the irremediable poverty of *mechanical* means. This "flat-footed" or, as the Romans called it, "planipes" dance, which has no jumps or movements on toe, is reduced to countless variations of basic runs and steps. Movements like thrusting a knee forward (around which the light fabric of her tunic rises like mist) or throwing a leg back (upsetting the pleats of her costume) are endlessly repeated. Often during her dance Duncan turns back her head and holds forth her arms with extended, pointing fingers—a typical gesture of ancient "dactylology." In general though, the artist uses the material of ancient dance only as far as her dilettantish technical abilities allow.

In the scene of the Elysian Fields Duncan brings a nuance of fragile, eighteenth-century grace into the image of the blessed shade, Orpheus' guide. And in the final glorification of the gods her hands, extended and trembling with joy, offer the Olympians lavish and exquisite gifts of thanks. The figurative strength of her gesture is such that the audience can see sacrificial flowers and vessels in her hands.

Of course, Duncan's mimed paraphrase hardly exhausts the content of *Orpheus*. The artist herself lately came to realize the conventional word-nature of gesture. In the actual event the sweet voice of the true Orpheus nonetheless sang in self-forgetfulness, intoned through a solo violin, while the mute dancer moved about the stage.

But despite her naive and limited concept of Orpheus, Duncan's performance was distinguished by nobility and deep tenderness.

The *Brahms Waltzes,* which made up the second half of the program, accords with the nature of Duncan's talent to a greater degree. The basis of her art does not lie in a conscious, formal creative approach, but in the peculiarities of her musical sensibility. The dance is *impressionistic* and evokes a sense of involuntary, sudden *improvisation*. The *Brahms Waltzes* are an example of this. To the first measures the dancer seems to be hesitating, even resisting the insinuation of the musical rhythm, until at length her movements become more definite and formed, and the whirlwind of the dance carries her away altogether. Above all, Duncan's art is *reproductive:* it is sound turned into motion. Her gestures often remind one of the instinctive dancing movements of a conductor on the podium.

The Brahms was followed by a Schubert encore. The somewhat naive but noble, penetrating lyricism of these dances, the charm of Duncan's genuine individuality dispelled the vague and at times tedious impression of *Orpheus.*

On the second evening, in Wagner's *Wesendonk Leider,* which date from the time of *Tristan,* the psychological *passivity* of Duncan's art was revealed even more clearly. In "Der Engel" her arms were crossed prayerfully and a smile radiated from her lips; in "Im Treibhaus," her arms enlaced, her torso (stiff, by the way, and not supple) was bent with exhaustion under the spell of sultriness; in "Schmerzen" her arms intertwined with a gesture of torment and self-defense; in "Träume," the dancer, lying on the ground, concretely represented one sleeping (the symbolism of Duncan's dance is always objective) and, raising herself up on her elbow, she joyfully immersed herself in the image of the magical dream.

Duncan uses these lieder as a prelude to *Isolde's Liebestod.* Here again her strength is focused on facial and manual mimicry. Her legs are motionless. Only occasionally does an impetuous gust seem to carry her a few steps ahead. And again, as in *Orpheus,* the artist—in a white chalmys with long sleeves, and with gestures of mournful tenderness—bends down over the body of her beloved until a storm of ecstasy straightens her bent stance and turns her clouded gaze aloft.

With the orchestra's every crescendo, she shakes her uplifted arms and finally throws them vigorously up and forward. This extreme tension is broken by the sinuous and smooth vibration of her horizontally-extended arms which seem to be carried by an invisible wave.

It goes without saying that this was not Isolde's tragic and majestic ascension; the dancer's movements only echoed an (imaginary) voice.

The Bacchanale in the Grotto of Venus from *Tannhäuser* is a complete failure. The performer does not have the ability to communicate the *multileveled* musical image in which melodic figures at times stand out distinctly and then slip back into the sea of orchestral polyphony. The Bacchanale cannot be realized without the contrapuntal opposition of separate groups within the dancing mass. That is why the artist, usually so attentive to the rhythm, here often contradicts it. Her whole image, which unites ripe femininity with ephebic masculinity, is alien to the music's raw, sensual charms. Here the crimson illumination of the stage and the blood-red tunic are also ineffectual.

The appearance of the *Three Graces* (the preparatory étude for this was Botticelli's *Primavera* which Duncan performed on previous occasions) is the pinnacle of her art. The dancing nymph reaches out her hand to an unseen friend and then she herself is suddenly the friend, a new dancer joining the harmonious khorovod. After her there appears a third. Duncan's fascination lies in this multiplicity of almost simultaneous incarnations, in this reduplication of personality. Elements of banal quick-change artistry are found alongside the surprise of authentic metamorphosis.

Such endeavors bring us close to the very essence of the dancer's artistic temperament.

Her psychological element is joy, the light intoxication brought on by the spring sun, by running freely, a gentle breeze playing with the pleats of her tunic. There is something bucolic about her. There is neither tragedy nor eroticism. There is, finally, no real femininity. In her, unpremeditated grace mingles with strength, the merriment of youth, any youth. And this is why this androgynous performer can be at once Orpheus and Eurydice, Narcissus and Daphne, Pan and Echo. And the symbolic embodiment of this duality of hers is *Ange avec violon*. These two evenings defined Duncan's significance for us. Undoubtedly the forms of her art have become familiar, but its emotional temperament will only sometimes awaken in us a response; her excitement often goes for naught. Nevertheless, her art is valuable as the manifestation of a unique personality, but this, in fact, exhausts her content.

This is a particular case, attractive but not important. Duncan's contribution to the general evolution of theatrical dance is scant and feeble.

It is not surprising that for Europe, for Germany, for countries that have no ballet, Duncan's appearance was a great event, a new revelation of the dance—that great lost happiness of body and soul. However, for Russian art as well, in which the great choreographic tradition of the "classical ballet" has been preserved, Duncan's appearance should have played an important role.

Meanwhile, as the leading talents of our choreographic stage take up and rashly rework Duncan's art and doctrine with Russian impulsiveness, Western aesthetic opinion, more perspicacious than ours, expounds a fundamental antithesis between the spirit of the Russian ballet and the important undertaking of this American artist. Despite the makeshift veneer of "modernism" which poorly conceals the Russian dancers' traditional habits, foreign critics see the inherent incompatibility of the two styles, the two artistic outlooks. The amalgamation of two alien creative elements will only confuse our critics for a while.

Here it seems proper to insist that the attitude of Western criticism toward the Russian ballet's campaigns has been reported back to us rather one-sidedly, simply as a wave of enthusiasm that seized the artists and aesthetes of Paris. But one can assert that the "Saisons Russes" captivated the likes of Auguste Rodin, Maurice Denis and Jacques-Emile Blanche, primarily as a revelation of a painterly-decorative order, as an avalanche of unbridled and farfetched colors. The living scenic action receded into the background.

It is precisely on the strength of this that Gordon Craig's *The Mask,* a purely theatrical publication, came out against the Russian designers and directors with extreme bitterness, even biting sarcasm. He identified the theatrical novelty of the "Russian plagiarists" as a deceptive recycling of the old, moribund pre-reform theater. Beneath the luxuriant raiment of exotic decors the principles of staging have remained unchanged. The implacable English theoreticians saw in the sensations of the new ballet nothing but a comedy in new guise.

Only on German soil was the question of ballet reform widely and passionately discussed. Here appeared the sharpest divergence of opinions and the battle between two polar conceptions: natural vs. artificial dance, Duncan vs. Anna Pavlova. For it was precisely in the performances of this ballerina, and not in Diaghilev's "Saisons," that the German critics saw the closest approximation to the essence of the Russian ballet.

We will visit each of the warring camps in turn. Hans Brandenburg's book *Der moderne Tanz* (Munich, 1914) cuts the Gordian knot with arrogant and rude straightforwardness. The book's first lines are devoted to Duncan's contribution as the source and origin of a newly recaptured art. With the very first words the knowingly "unartistic" Russian ballet is scornfully dismissed. The concluding remarks return to Duncan's significance, this time not only to assert it, but to delimit it. Brandenburg is convinced of the plastic "poverty of her richness" and fears her saving simplicity will degenerate into a style, conventional in its own terms. He finds complete "inadequacy" vis-à-vis the musical text in her interpretation of Wagner's *Wesendonk Lieder* and also mentions her extreme paucity of imagination and inordinate sentimentality. But he insists to the full on the decisive, crucial significance of Duncan's method. Her name is the banner and symbol of the whole renewal of dance.

Parallel to this apologia of Duncan's innovation, a special chapter contains a reprisal against the Russian ballet. The German critic disputes its right to exist, resorting to the usual, typical arguments: acrobatics, affectation, immorality. "The modern audience," Brandenburg suggests, "is not in a position to exclude from its consciousness the work of Duncan and Jaques-Dalcroze, and is henceforth unable to give itself up to the narcotic seduction of affectation." The verdict on the Russian ballet has been pronounced. Was Brandenburg not among those good citizens of Munich who hissed Anna Pavlova for her performance in a classical *pas de deux,* just as once, in the anecdote that so struck Pushkin, Salieri hissed Mozart?

However, it was in the German milieu, and precisely at its cultural zenith that Duncan's undertaking met its most serious rebuff. Germany's best critic, Meier-Graefe, in *The Spanish Journey,* [*Spanische Reise,* Berlin: 1910], jeers in passing at her "skipping like a governess." No less strict is Professor Bie,[4] that thorough explorer of the history of dance:

Miss Duncan, as might only have been expected, foundered on her lack of culture. Prévost knew how to dance, Hamilton wanted to dance, Fuller didn't even want to, but Duncan could not. She danced without tights but her body was too flimsy a column. She did not smile the stylized smile of a ballerina, but her features wore the expression of a governess. She tried to link artistic poses through animated movements, but her torso was completely undeveloped. . . . She danced to familiar classical music, but her incorrect interpretation of the rhythm revealed her extreme unmusicality. She danced Couperin and Chopin, Gluck and Greek choruses, but she could not reform ballet for us.

Pavlova's appearance, on the other hand, had been a revelation for this erudite Berliner: he, who had written a thick book on dance, for the first time realized what dance was.

But nowhere was this revelation of the lost and newly-recovered art of the dance more fully reflected than in Ernest Schur's elegant book *Der moderne Tanz* [Munich, 1910]. In his survey this sensitive writer-impressionist takes as his point of departure a withering critique of what he knew under the heading "ballet." With great sarcasm he speaks out against dance "hardened in schematic formalism," against "grotesque" tutus and soulless movement. These tutus seem to tear the body in two. The innovators' aim is clear: "To free dance from the yoke of its past, to rehabilitate nature, to replace constraint with freedom." The ultimate goal: "Once again, through what is natural, to arrive at style, at art." This conviction, to which even our persecutors of the ballet would willingly subscribe, leads Schur to the happy acknowledgment of Duncan's initiative: "She was the first who searched. She freed herself. She once again experienced the dance. This is the source of her exultation." It is true that she, "like an Englishwoman, was denied original creation. But rather, she asks, 'What can I use?' Where she went wrong was that instead of the athleticism she knew well, she cultivated an unknown, ancient ideal." Be that as it may, a beginning was made; her work was cut out. The groundwork was laid for further development. This much Brandenburg also affirms. And here Schur amuses himself sketching Duncan's followers and heirs. In the endeavors of Ruth St. Denis or the Wiesenthal Sisters he seeks material for the aesthetics of renewed dance . . . until the phenomenon of the Russian (classical) ballet bursts upon his imagination like a streak of lightning. Why is this impression so tremendous? "A feeling of continuity was awakened. Naturalness once again deceived us," admits the German critic. "The futility and the insignificance of all the various debates brought us back to our senses, back to the blessings of tradition, to convention. At that instant the Russians came and showed us what was missing. They came just in time." Schur's enlightenment and repentance has Pavlova's example as its source. The self-imposed limits of dance schemes, the significance of body discipline, elevating spontaneity to the level of expressivity became clear to him. He regrets that the innovators have lost their flair for symbolic gesture. "We nowadays banish the beauty of expressive, stylized movement from dance itself, and thus ban from art the only significant thing: art itself. We save only that which is insignificant. The movements from which Pavlova's art is composed are as beautiful as style in a sculpture, as rhythm in a building. They are revelations of hidden beauty. They are something symbolic—a logical testimony to the perfection of the universe."

I cite these words with emotion, so well do they correspond to that apperception of the metaphysical nature of classical dance, the visible herald from the world of ideas, which has stirred and exalted me for many long years. How could we exchange these secret voices, which sound distinctly in ballet's mute symbolism, for the aesthetic diversions of the new ballet masters, for the playthings of precocious snobbism and restless frivolity? Perhaps faith in a foreigner's opinion will help the ever "advanced" and susceptible to lure our audience into valuing not the Russian ballet's tinseled decor and exotic trappings, but the golden essence of the art.

.

Notes to Chapter 2

1. Isadora Duncan (1877–1927) made her first trip to Russia in 1904 where she created a great controversy between the supporters of classical ballet and the advocates of ballet reform, notably Fokine. She returned in 1907, 1912 and again in 1921 when she founded a school and married the poet Sergei Esenin. See: Ilya Ilich Schneider, *Isadora Duncan, The Russian Years,* trans. David Magarshack (New York: Harcourt, Brace and World, Inc., 1968) and Gordon McVay, *Isadora and Esenin* (Ann Arbor: Ardis, 1980).
2. See: Arkadii Georgievich Gornfel'd, *Knigi i liudi* (St. Petersburg: Zhizn', 1908).
3. A reference to Goethe's poem "The Pariah."
4. See: Oskar Bie, *Gesellschaftstanz der Renaissance,* 1903; *Das Ballett,* [1905]; *Der Tanz als Kunstwerk,* [1905]; *Der Tanz* 1906; *Tanzmusik* [1905?]; *Der moderne Tanz,* 1920; *Bühne, Ball und Bänkel,* [1923].

CHAPTER THREE

A Subject
of Debate

I
TWO AESTHETICS

C L A S S I C A L B A L L E T, which arose as far back as the seventeenth century, reached its maturity during the Romantic era, and was bequeathed to us Russians through the genius of Marius Ivanovich Petipa and his associates, develops fairy tale, historical, conventional and allegorical subjects in the hybrid form of dance combined with pantomime.

The mime side, though completely stylized, expresses the characters' dramatized emotional states. They are simple but strong: a mute gesture is, perhaps, the most powerful exponent of elementary emotions. But dramatic tension, which can only be truly resolved by the liberating word, is dissipated into the realm of fantasy when

37

joined by dance which is almost completely free of concrete motifs.

Ballet subjects are often constructed in such a way that the characters are living an ethereal life along with their real one.

The Bayadère in the well-known ballet, when poisoned by her rival, continues her existence—freed from earth-bound materiality—as a shade; deceived Giselle turns into a mermaid-wili; Raymonda, in a reverie, appears before her very self in the form of a dream-like apparition, and so on.

Slipping into a fantastic plane, the heroine forsakes natural movement. She rises on *pointe,* onto the tips of her pointed toes. This is really neither a step nor a leap; it is a special form of movement which transcends the laws of equilibrium, earth's gravity, the mechanical habits of everyday movement. The ballerina no longer belongs to the earth, her kingdom is ethereal space, the sphere of freed fantasy where "all is light and oblivion." One of the dances Pavlova included in her London performances was *The Dying Swan,* composed by Fokine to Saint-Saëns' music. In its very simplicity this dance is the crowning illustration of the strength of free expressivity—an inherent quality of pure classical dance, devoid of concrete, dramatic gesticulation.

Her swift, short steps on extended toes, the rhythmic trembling of her tensed muscles creates the unmistakable impression of a desire to rise, take wing, fly up and free herself from the yoke of agonizing experience, whereas the constrained movements of her arms, interlaced over her head like wings that have been shot, create the tragic impression of the impossibility of flight, of vain effort, despair. And when at the end of the dance she falls onto one knee, lowering her head and her powerlessly-interlaced arms, you feel you have witnessed the completed drama of a free spirit held back by earthly traction—a drama which could serve as the epigraph to Mallarmé's poem:

"Tout son col secouera cette blanche agonie."[1]

But the impression's leaden weight is dispelled by the thought that a single jump, the merest *cabriole* might return the wounded bird to the air.

A special type of attire corresponds to this imagined existence. The short ballet tunic—the "tutu"—which has called forth such endless censure, is a light, short outfit made of pleated white gauze giving complete freedom of movement to the legs and arms, apparent stability to the body and increasing that impression of pure butterfly airiness that dance on *pointe* creates. The tunic's extensive surface produces an instant of relative immobility, a contrast which emphasizes the movement being performed. The flesh-colored tights (whose origin is attributed to bourgeois hypocrisy) and the blunt slipper, which evens out the contour of the foot, make the impression of the movements seem more precise and finished. The two elements of classical ballet are actually not distinguished as strictly as one might conclude from what I have said. They are mixed and combined in various ways. The so-called *pas d'action* and mime scenes are often interrupted and illustrated by dances.

The kingdom of "classical" dance forms is so extensive that you cannot take stock of it or describe it. Only a ballet master's vast experience can embrace all the combinations of movements and all the positions of the arms, legs and torso that are possible within the limits of its technique. Such a description of classical dance forms is beyond the scope of the present undertaking. But the old ballet is not confined to the two instances I have noted: pantomime and classical dance. It also draws its content and coloration from ethnological observation, national and folk (so-called "character") dances.

Creative fantasy is not dependent on the strict rules of causality. The librettist can choose his pretext at will—a wedding, betrothal, religious festival—to motivate the so-called divertissement, made up predominantly of character dances. Petipa used choreographic forms from Spain and Hungary, India and Persia, France under the *Ancien Régime,* Russia of legendary times. There are ballets, such as *Don Quixote* or *The Little Humpbacked Horse* (by Saint-Léon), that are completely based on national themes yet which do not violate ballet's basic duality: the uniting of action and classical dance.

Not satisfied with borrowing of national forms directly, Petipa often translated them into the strict language of the classical style, as in the *grand pas hongrois* from *Raymonda.* Another example showing national dance penetrated by the ample, strict classical manner is the Russian Dance from *The Little Humpbacked Horse* which we mentioned earlier.

I have had to present here only the most schematic outline of the structure of the old ballet, its physics and metaphysics, and indicate its inner meaning only in its most general features. But it seems to me that if the striving for the "historical method" in art, which we now generally observe, should lead us to any remnant at all of such an inexhaustible richness as was the old ballet, we should exert all efforts to restore this lost source of the water of life—which, miraculously, has been preserved here in Russia, and which too many of us are ready to muddy up and let evaporate completely. What else, then, are those paths of reform and renewal upon which Fokine's enthusiasm for the mimed character of ancient dance and the idiosyncrasies of his peculiar artistic temperament have caused him to embark?

Having renounced classical dance, which is conventional and abstract, in the name of scenic and psychological realism, Fokine had to turn, on the one hand, to the ancient world and on the other, to a unique living source, to "character" dances, to daily life and history, to the dances and rituals of all manner of tribes and peoples (which, in most cases, have become extinct since peoples today do not dance) while salon and court dances, *danses de société,* the *Ancien Régime*'s minuets and pavanes, the polonaises of the Restoration and all that, played a greater role in the old ballet and do not respond to the new canon of choreography. The living forms of national dances—the Hungarian czardas, Spanish fandango or jaleo—also had to yield their places to the East and to the ancient world.

Hence the predominance of ethnography and archaeology in Fokine's work. It is no accident that his great artistic achievement—the Polovetsian Dances from *Prince Igor*—in which there foams the primitive, bellicose and passionate blood of a wild horde—was achieved in collaboration with Roerich, the painter-archaeologist.

Egypt, Persia, Ancient Greece and legendary Russia have each paid tribute to the ballet master. Even in his first important work, *Egyptian Nights,* which was rooted in historical and ethnological sources, Fokine attempts to transcend the old forms. But this composition, monotonous in its dramatic development, is actually an unbroken divertissement put together out of the most heterogeneous and incongruous fragments whose common pretext is a temple festival in Cleopatra's honor. Here, despite the absence of white tunics and symmetrical adagios, there is still no transcendence of the old ballet duality that we have emphasized, but only a transparent mask of novelty.

Old ballet divertissements usually end with a so-called "coda." The coda is a short repetition of the *pas* executed by all the performers of the divertissement's different dances, who join in one after the other. At the end, the whole mass of dancers assembles on the proscenium, facing the audience, each one meanwhile repeating some basic movement of his dance, concentrating it to its essence to the final chords of the music.

In nearly every one of Fokine's ballets there is a moment where all the participants, irrespective of their earlier roles, join hands and form a long chain—a farandole—which closes up into concentric circles and carries on to an ever-accelerating tempo. This cotillion figure, which we have described both in connection with *Cleopatra* and *Sheherazade* and which occurs, with few variations, in *all* Fokine's works, is nothing else but a modified coda.

The coda in classical ballet forms as if in single file before the audience. This is, perhaps, "unnatural" from the dramatic standpoint, but it allows the audience to grasp the totality of the movement being performed at a single glance. Fokine's "realistic ballet," which preserves its final *tutti,* gives it the "natural" character of the uncontrolled, orgiastic whirling of a crowd—intoxicated by the dance and by god—dancing, of course, not for the audience but for themselves. This contiguous, indecipherable mass, this tangle of bodies rushing about was interesting when Fokine first presented it, but when stubbornly repeated in every ballet, on any pretext, it eventually became tiresome. . . .

Fokine proceeds even further in the pseudo-dramatization of ballet in *Sheherazade* where, despite all its colorful charm, there is neither dramatic movement nor dance "in the ballet sense of the word," as our critics would put it—that is to say, no dancing at all. Its subject is "jealousy" personified by the traditional "Sultan, somber and pitiful under the gold of his caftan."* *Sheherazade* marks a transitional step in quest of pantomime, the form of drama with which Fokine is decisively identified since *Firebird,* at least officially.

And in fact, as the vehicle for logical, uninterrupted dramatic development, ballet approaches pure pantomime by nature.

A special quality of the ballet master's artistic temperament led him to *eroticism* as a source of dramatic content.

In *Sheherazade* and *Cleopatra* the action is either monotonous or (in the case of the latter) completely episodic without a hint of inner continuity. Instead, the ballet master lavishly filled all the gaps and

---

*La jalousie—un sultan sombre
Et pitieux sous l'or du caftan . . . P. Verlaine

breaks with erotic visions. Not for nothing did Fokine so eagerly seek material in Eastern dances which to a notable extent culminate in a simulation of physical love.

His *Sheherazade,* and in part the Bacchanale in the Grotto of Venus, writhe in continuous passionate convulsions. Here he strives deliberately toward some type of realism. The gestures and mime of the erotic experience are presented so concretely that there is almost no room for the audience's sexual imagination, and the artistic value of the conception is destroyed. Intoxication by passion and blood is the action's primary motive force. The bloody orgy at the end—with someone leaning over the balustrade and pouring out blood—is completely in keeping with the Negroes and odalisques who contort themselves on the harem pillows in *Sheherazade.*

But don't attribute motives out of the *lex Heinze* to my critique: it just seems to me that generally the erotic demands very restrained treatment on the stage. Doubtless, the very fact of a love experience, its origin and development, the struggle for its realization, its individual character may be interesting and indeed significant as theater. But the purely physical instant, monotonous and lacking psychic nuances, lies outside the realm of theater illusion. Turning the stage into a tremendous boudoir is only a needless, monstrous pleonasm and destroys the inner economy of the action.

The vulgarized Dionysius of the Bacchanale and the "Venus vulgivaga" of Fokine's erotic fantasies have only crept in as by-products of the disintegration of "classical" ballet's apollonian beauty, whose watchword might well have been Nietzsche's words about freeing the soul from the oppression and tension of dramatic experience through imagining ideal beauty: *Erlösung durch den Schein.* We saw how Fokine, in pursuit of literal realism in ballet, attempted in the first place to lay a foundation for the structure of the ballet in the concrete motivation of every movement, and secondly, to replace fantastic invention with authentic experiences, whose source he found particularly in the erotic.

The third point particularly emphasized by the "new ballet's" propagandists is the "group principle." "Group action," about which several years ago all and sundry were holding forth, is ostensibly drawn from the depths of the Russian national soul (like the Slavophile's "tribal community" of old) and in theatrical terms the predominance of the "ensemble" has come to the fore as a basic principle of the new ballet.

Actually, subjugating the self-sufficient personality of the soloist to the disciplined mass as a collective character is not only not the essence of Fokine's productions, but in many ways contradicts it. This discipline of masses moving symmetrically to a single rhythm is one of the fundamental achievements of "classical ballet," as may be seen in the second act of *Giselle,* in *La Bayadère* and in nearly all the ballets of the contemporary repertoire. Always, in its most diverse manifestations, "classical" ballet has been the national standard-bearer of the aesthetic principle of "unity within diversity." Fokine, however, in his famous khorovods, to which I have referred repeatedly, *individualizes* the role of each performer, granting each unit of the ensemble all possible freedom of movement and gesture. This is why his Bacchanale is not a hieratic dance or a divine service in which every movement is governed by ritual and eurythmy, but is rather the nocturnal wandering of an intoxicated crowd in the mountains. This may be a leaf from the mysterious customs of Ancient Greece, but in any case is not a restoration of the "group principle" of ancient choric dances.

Fokine's khorovod is the breakdown of the classical ensemble. On the whole, one can hardly accuse him of neglecting the role of the individual in his ballets. On the contrary, in composing his ballets he has skillfully taken account of the individual particularities of their future performers. It is true that he has abolished the complex form of the *pas de deux,* which is incompatible with ballet realism; he has done away with all the adagios and pizzicatos. Experience has shown that *Egyptian Nights* faded once and for all without Pavlova's astounding pliancy and that the ballet *Chopiniana* concentrates best of all around the elastic Nijinsky, and so on.

Fokine's ballets exist by virtue of individual artistic personalities that have been schooled in the old ballet, by grace of that very school he so insistently tried to defeat and whose form he uses only in an abbreviated and impoverished way.

All the performers in *Sheherazade* or *Firebird* have withstood the protracted ordeal of classical ballet training, which developed in them all the possibilities of movement, a lightness that overcomes gravity and a strength that doesn't know fatigue. Most of all, it developed that unity of style, that uncanny uniformity that is so brutally shattered by the introduction of any extraneous element. It is hard to imagine a cruder error in taste than the participation of a certain dilettante *danseuse* in the Parisian performances.[2] She was completely at variance with the other performers who had passed through our ballet's rigorous course of study.

Thus Fokine works "with all expenses paid." A connoisseur of the old ballet, an excellent classical dancer himself, who has given tradition its due in *Chopiniana, Le Pavillon d'Armide* and in the not uninteresting suite he composed to Tchaikovsky's *The Seasons* for his ballet school examination, Fokine even in his innovative works often makes use of technical material from the old ballet.

Almost all the *Egyptian Nights* are danced on *pointe;* the amazing jumps of Nijinsky as the Slave are more the reason for this ballet's success than his monotonous and mannered dramatic qualities.

Fokine has repudiated the old forms even more decisively in his latest productions; but along with this, the choreographic element is truncated more and more, as we have demonstrated with regard to *Firebird.*

The new ballet's latest attainment is the richness of pictorial impression.

II

BALLET, PAINTING, MUSIC

The old ballet, with its pink and white ballerina figures, never got beyond naive scenic splendor in the matter of decor. Conventional set design, timidly pretending to historical or archaeological accuracy, provided its usual frame.

The costumes of the cavaliers and character dancers were distinguished by a motley completely without regard for color combinations. There was no question of a general color harmony. The first attempts to improve this area were the elegant productions of *Die Puppenfee* and Glazunov's *The Seasons* by Bakst and Legat, and the revival of *Talisman* for which Prince Shervashidze designed beautiful costumes.

Diaghilev's productions during the "Saisons Russes" in Paris, which I have described in detail, were a dazzling and noisy victory for Russian stage design—a victory whose heroes were Alexandre Benois, Golovin and, mainly, Bakst. Not so long ago (1911) [sic][3], a prominent representative of our school of painting, in an article evaluating a production of Molière's *Don Juan* at the Alexandrinsky

Theatre, expressed sincere though belated, and not complete, remorse at the ambiguous and dangerous role that painting and its representatives have played among the martyrs of our dramatic stage.

The article was entitled "Ballet at the Alexandrinka." According to the author, Alexandre Benois, the predominance of painting, the cult of the beautiful moment and "wispish" arabesque should not be accommodated to the drama, which bears the baggage of mankind's ideas and expresses its psychological depths.

Here the question is of course not one of ideas or of the soul "which it is finally time to consider." Painting seems to us to be as fully capable as the other arts to bear an ideological or psychological message. But the fact is the painterly side of a production contradicts drama's basic characteristic and essence: movement, development, dynamic. We have no intention of stirring up the classic debate on the limits of painting, but will only recall that, by its very essence, it is static. Existing in two dimensions, it is immobile in time and space, in which the rhythm of movement, music and words lives and develops infinitely.

Painterly rhythm can only be expressed by a harmonic combination of lines or points—a combination which records a single instant of movement but which, of course, does not stop the audience from adding to it in their imagination, either by analogy or from experience, the preceding or following moments, thus destroying the unity of the purely pictorial impression. Just as a hundred dots placed next to each other do not create a line, so a hundred drawings depicting consecutive instants (be they ever so brief) or movements cannot represent movement itself. Baudelaire's allegory of beauty might serve as the motto for *pictorial* impression: *Je hais le mouvement qui déplace les lignes*—I hate the movement that displaces the lines.

These elementary considerations demonstrate that dance and painting are only close as objects of audience perception. Besides Fokine's unnecessary, superficial and jejune attempt to dramatize ballet, another weak spot in his compositions is precisely this predominance of the pictorial. If all the action of *Sheherazade* and *Firebird* could have been replaced by a skillfully-arranged series of living pictures, the audience might have been at leisure to discern more freely the extraordinary beauties of the set design and the ornamentation lavished by Bakst and Golovin. Sometimes all the mad moving about on stage seems like nothing more than an annoying commotion and distraction—the more so as giving up the skimpy choreographic content of these ballets does not seem like much of a sacrifice. The victory of Russian painting at the Grand Opéra cost ballets like these dearly. Meanwhile, a lot of work lies ahead for our artists associated with the ballet. Almost all the old ballets are in need of new productions. I already mentioned some successful ventures in this area. And when our artists do take on this auxiliary, "applied" but essential role, let them be met by the same honorable but cruel fate to which the author of *The Republic* condemns poets, crowning them with laurels and sending them into exile. Otherwise, ballet may be threatened by the same fate as befell the dramatic theater.

The last aspect of ballet reform that is associated with the innovations of Duncan and Fokine is the vexed question of music. We know Miss Duncan has utilized nearly all of musical literature as background for her dances, from Chopin, Beethoven and Schubert to Johann Strauss. Her most successful choices have been Gluck (whose *Iphigenia in Aulide* she completely translated into the language of choreography and mime) and eighteenth-century composers such as Rameau and Couperin with their simple, clearly defined rhythm.

We are clearly indebted to Duncan's initiative for the emergence of analogous devices in our new ballet.

In the majority of cases, the musical accompaniment—one of the weakest elements of classical ballet—is of a routine nature, devoid of individual features. This music was manufactured in mass production by the official composers Minkus and Pugni. Its only virtue is its aptness for balletic forms in conformity with its technical role—that of creating the rhythmic line and precise melodic pattern for the dancing to follow.

But even the masterpieces of musical accompaniment for dance (Tchaikovsky's three ballets, Glazunov's brilliant but uneven *Raymonda,* his *Seasons,* the ballets of Delibes and Lalo) do not suit today's taste in music which fluctuates between the complex forms of the post-Wagnerian tendency, the ethereality of Impressionism and the hieratic severity of Bach and pre-classic music.

Traditional ballet music corresponds more or less to the recitative-arioso style in opera. The melody of a balletic adagio has a finished, rounded form, which is separate from the general organic continuity of the music, and which breaks up into two or more symmetrically arranged parts which are regularly repeated. The thematic independence of a balletic adagio or pizzicato and the parallelism of its parts brings them close to an operatic aria, whereas the accompanying mimed scenes somewhat approach a recitative.

This form, which contradicts the ideal of musical drama and today's musical ideals in general, is so closely bound up with classical ballet's choreographic model that one cannot get away from it. If one were to get rid of the insignificant music of *La Bayadère* or *Le Corsaire,* one would have to give up the corresponding dances, created by a great artist, which is what Marius Petipa was. The only palliative would be a more refined reorchestration of the old scores which might lend them a certain aural charm.

Fokine's art, not bound by the canons of conventional balletic forms, naturally tried to find an "adequate," if it may be so expressed, musical form for itself. After a whole series of attempts wherein the ballet master made his work dependent on ready-made musical forms (and we have seen that not one of these attempts could be called completely successful), the new ballet tried to create for itself the musical atmosphere it needed. First was Tcherepnine's interesting if unpretentious *Le Pavillon d'Armide* in which reminiscences of the earlier treatments of Tasso's sorceress by Lully and Gluck were cloaked in the complex and lively raiment of contemporary instrumentation. This was followed by Igor Stravinsky's *Firebird,* which we have already described. We noted then that the merits of this ballet lay completely outside the realm of choreography which requires clarity of rhythmic structure above all else.

Thus the new ballet has not resolved the dilemma to which "classical ballet" had reconciled itself. We have tried to trace the route taken by Fokine's ballet reforms: 1) *a gradual movement away from the old ballet's duality toward a unified action, from choreography to pure pantomime—in the name of the fiction of consistent realism;* 2) *further, the subordination of dramatic movement to the static principle of pure representation;* 3) *finally, the complication of musical rhythm and the replacement of the musical accompaniment by the autonomous form of a symphonic suite.*

It seems clear to me that despite all the new ballet's pictorial and other beauties, despite all the splendor of its diverse impressions (both visual and musical) with which it showers us, despite all the ballet master-innovator's energy, gifts and personal charm, the path he and his associates have chosen for the Parisian *Festspeile* is the path of ballet's *suicide* on the public stage. And were it not for that great conservative force, the classical pedagogy of our ballet school, there's no telling how far this new ballet would travel along the path of degeneracy.

However, one should not exaggerate the dangers of the new course. You cannot discount the quantity of new experience that the collaboration of so many talented people must bring about. And one shouldn't even talk about the need for artistic repression. Classical ballet can afford to be magnanimous toward its younger rival because its old Romantic sun has perhaps never shone so brightly. Its rays permeate Mathilda Kchessinska's interpretive genius, her perfect art with its infinitely complex technique and the clarity of sudden revelation; the poetic charm that enriches Anna Pavlova with an aura of ineffably-aerial Romanticism; and the confident skill of Olga Preobrajenska and Ekaterina Geltzer. There is no such blossoming of talents among us in any other area of art. Along with those I have named and with Vera Trefilova, who untimely left our stage (and for whom dance was as music for Mozart—a natural element), I could continue this "catalogue of heroes" infinitely, but names in themselves convey so little. . . .

If such is the case, what is all the shouting about and why the sharpness of critical debate? It is just the particular immanent nature of the choreographic theater.

The works of dance art differ from those of playwrights in that they have only scenic existence, only a fleeting reality on the boards. Outside this framework, a ballet by the best master is but a shadow of a shade. The thing that forms its living soul cannot be read in a book, gleaned from a vocal score. Its libretto as written is no more than a conventional schema of action, banal in its nudity. Its music, taken by itself, creates only the emotional and rhythmic background for unrealized sculptural and dynamic images (although it is able to preserve its specific *hors-théâtre* worth, a value which is not complete since "dance music" is by its very nature an "applied" art).

Ballet's objective is the creation of forms in the eyes of the spectators through living, human movements. As soon as the curtain falls these forms are dissolved until the next realization. One's abstract conception of them has no aesthetic reality. It is not without reason that one of the newest critics maintains paradoxically that dance figures lack the necessary conditions of art because they are transient.

These figures seem to retain the possibility of life so long as they are preserved in the artists' visual, musical (the types of associations vary) and, mainly, "motor" memories. If there is a prolonged interval, these grow weak and are lost. Attempts to preserve and restore the priceless legacy of Marius Petipa and Lev Ivanov have been and continue to be made automatically, so to speak, using the conventional notation of *pas* and *tempi*. In this way one can collect and fix each little bone and each muscle of the artistic organism as if it were an artificial cadaver for an anatomy lesson. But it is possible to breathe life into this "Homunculus" only when the performers themselves preserve a living memory of the original production. Thus the only way to preserve the precious choreographic works of the past is to continue their performance traditions without interruption. Thus is the danger of departures and experiments. The forms of dance must be guarded vigilantly just like the fire at the vestal sanctuary. Once extinguished, it will not flare up again.

Notes to Chapter 3

1. From Mallarmé's poem "Le vierge, le viveau et le bel aujourd'hui."
2. A reference to Ida Rubinstein.
3. See: "Balet v Aleksandrinke—O postanovke Meierkhol'dom 'Don Zhuana' " in *Rech'*, 19 November 1910.

CHAPTER FOUR

The Ballets Russes at the Théâtre des Champs Elysées (1913)

I
NIJINSKY'S BALLETS:
LE SACRE DU PRINTEMPS, JEUX

I T would be wrong to contend that up to now the Ballets Russes in Paris has not known failure. One has but to remember the taciturn, restrained but merciless rejection of *Giselle* three years ago, the obvious inability of *Le Pavillon d'Armide* to hold its ground for long in a repertoire for foreign consumption, the polite indifference with which the public greeted the pallid, quickly worn out *Thamar*—a vapid repetition of Fokine's earlier inspirations. But the noisy failure of *Le Sacre du Printemps* was, despite the undoubted *succès de scandal* as expressed by the extraordinary attendance, a genuine catastrophe.

51

The loud protests stirred up by the earlier production of *Jeux* by Claude Debussy, Nijinsky and Bakst was but a prelude to the storm that raged around Stravinsky's ballet.

Now that a few years have passed and one can begin to see the events of that remarkable summer in perspective, it seems to me that the violent indignation from the parterre and boxes was not only created by the artistic shortcomings of the new ballets, but to a greater degree by certain psychological characteristics of the Parisian cultured set, primarily their innate conservatism. Fokine's ballet style, once it met with their acceptance and approval, managed to acquire over the last several years their sanction and the stability of a new choreographic tradition. And this is why they rose up against an insult to aesthetic habits so recently acquired in the realm of dance—habits so blatantly flouted by Nijinsky's daring. In addition, the performers of *Jeux* appeared in white knit athletic outfits, and this painfully offended French formalism with its pedantic sense of propriety.

For they are unswerving in their differentiation of scenic genres and their separation of high and low styles of staging. The appearance of figures with the typical exterior characteristics of a "variety" theater on the lyrical stage offended them as something verging on the indecent.

We shall leave aside, however, the curious circumstances surrounding the fall of *Le Sacre du Printemps* in order to clarify its purely artistic basis. To do so, I must turn partly to the impressions I noted down that summer, especially as Stravinsky's music in its scenic garments has remained inaccessible and unknown to the Russian public.

In the conception of Roerich, the librettist and designer, the chaotic, mysterious, ancient face of primeval humanity—grimacing in transcendent, elemental horror before the secret of things—shows distinctly through the transparent historical facade of pre-Christian Russia.

These "Scenes of Pagan Russia" do not have much of a subject in terms of psychological development, for the spiritual sufferings of primitive peoples are too vague and rudimentary for that. For this reason the action lacks structure.

And there is no such structure in Stravinsky's music either: built partly on folk song motifs (Stravinsky generally refrains from thematic invention), it is extremely fragmentary. There are parts in which the same short melodic figure of two to four notes is repeated over and over again with monotonous persistence. It's true that a similar underlying rhythmic uniformity can be found, for example, even in such exalting and universally acclaimed a masterpiece as Beethoven's Seventh Symphony, but there the rhythmic figure appears in countless melodic transformations. The single, willful dynamic impulse is decked out in all the complexity and whimsy of emotional life in full flower.

Meanwhile, in Stravinsky's score, his meager themes are almost completely undeveloped. The musical phrase is repeated ad infinitum with sluggish and tedious persistence. Suddenly, without any transition, a new theme interrupts only to again appear in an unchanging aspect while we search in vain for a familiar harmonious parallelism of parts.

But let us return to Roerich's conception, insofar as the audience can figure it out.

In the first scene, "The Kiss of the Earth," Roerich recreates aspects of ancient life and cult, the springtime ecstasies of shamans, imaginary ceremonies, bowing down to the earth, the games of "rival tribes". . . .

Amid bright greening hills with deeply disquieting round masses, under a beetling stone-like sky (the usual scenario for the artist's visions of the past) youths and maidens give themselves up to mystical dances. At the end, the most ancient of the old men kisses the earth. We have never seen anything like these dances. As if under hypnosis, monotonously and darkly, the same coarse, constrained and obtusely-stubborn movements are repeated until a spasmodic jolt breaks the stupefyingly-uniform tenor of their movements.

As if depersonalized by the cult, knowing no individual impulse, the dancers move in locked groups, shoulder to shoulder.

Some kind of irresistible compulsion prevails over them omnipotently, twisting their limbs, weighing down upon their bent necks. It seems that other types of movement, more free or harmonious, are forbidden as if blasphemous.

All this seems completely plausible to me on the psychological or genre plane. I can admit the assumption and willingly trust the librettist's extraordinary archaeological flair, and can believe that the spring rites of pagan Russia were, down to the smallest details, just as they were on stage at the Champs Elysées. But it is precisely in this archaeological exactitude of the production that I see the authors' fundamental delusion. The rules of scenic reality are hardly the same as the particulars of primeval ethnography. Our courageous novelty seekers have repeated here the old mistakes of naturalism, now moribund in the theater.

It is no wonder that the ponderous mystical torpor that commands the dancing groups creates painful, acute, even psychological displeasure in the audience.

The sources of this age-old delusion, which infects today's most accomplished artists of the stage (Russian artists) with its charms, lurks in Stravinsky's eccentric, demonic music (there are many sonorities in it familiar from *Petrushka*) which pierces the ear with unbearable dissonances and heavy, imperious rhythms.

I beg the reader's indulgence in leaving to the professional musicians the technical evaluation of the novelty (the simultaneous combination of two different keys) or, perhaps, the anarchy of musical style in this unprecedented score, especially as St. Petersburg has already had the opportunity to acquaint itself with the work in concert performance.

But if Stravinsky's innovation has been an unsuccessful attempt (and this seems likely), then what a brilliant failure it is! The musical fabric is so dense, his creative will is so intense and individual, his immersion in the servile, pathetic primitive soul is so complete. It is true that the wonderful decorative colors of *Fireworks* and *Firebird* have been replaced by the coarse rags of barbarian chanting. The woodwind instruments, flutes and oboes sometimes sound as artless as the reed pipes of the earliest nomads while the bassoons sound like drilled skulls in the cruel, dexterous fingers of a cannibal-improviser.

I don't know anything more recherché than this Hottentot music!

This is roughly what I wrote under the direct influence of those memorable performances. It is curious to note that my attempt to come to grips with the extraordinary impressions of Stravinsky's music called forth the reproach of a literary critic from a highly respected "thick journal" who said the Futurists had "dragged me along" since I was able to accept the art I myself had labeled "Hottentot."

I rebuff this reproach. I approved neither of Hottentotism nor of the composer's intentions nor of the forms he created. I was only carried away—this once—by Stravinsky's irresistible musical personality, the charm of his talent and will, pedantic and eccentric at the same time though it be.

But it was in the way the ballet master interpreted the music and the way in which he subordinated the performers to it that the fatal error and the highly instructive mistake of this production was to be found. The only rational goal of the movements he created was the realization of the rhythm. The rhythm, such as it was in his conception, was the single enormous force restraining the primitive soul.

The dancers embody the relative length and force of the sound and the acceleration and slowing of the tempo in the schematic gymnastics of their movement: they bend and straighten their knees, raise and lower their heels, stamp in place, forcefully beating out the accented notes. This is the whole standard pedagogical arsenal of teaching rhythmic gymnastics according to the Jaques-Dalcroze system. Entirely rational and expedient in their place, these schemes for movement, when placed on stage, lose their original "applied" meaning as validated through experience.

By some inscrutable lapse in taste and understanding, the plastic, psychological and symbolic content of the dance was replaced by these auxiliary textbook formulas for movement.

Nijinsky, in his one-sided enthusiasm, lost sight of the fact that rhythm is only a naked form, only the measure of movement in time, devoid of autonomous content. But all the sculptural aspects were sacrificed to it.

And thus throughout the production, wherever the whirling of the savages, possessed by the Spring and intoxicated by the diety, turned into a tedious demonstration of rhythmic gymnastics and wherever shamans and possessed beings started to "walk the notes" and "syncopate," there you had the origin of the psychological downfall of the whole idea and, most inevitably, a comical sense of bewilderment in the audience. The naive "amateur" quality of the scheme could not but alienate them.

It does not seem that this new rhythmic formalism has a right to stifle pure movement; on its own it makes little impression.

The choreographic example of the eighteenth century prescribed that we feel rhythm without emphasizing it. Now it has been forgotten. It seems the theoreticians and propagandists could not wait to forge a "free" dance constrained by irrelevancies for the greater glory of a contrived distraction into the art of theatrical dance.

The worst evil in our cultural life is this: an overflow of frivolity and simplemindedness, the urge to vulgarize, and the quick and easy assimilation of superficial effects. Thus, for example, Fokine's endeavors in recreating ancient dance are erroneous not so much as pursuits in themselves, but as the overly rash and hasty assimilation of the subject; there is no sense of immersion, no real knowledge, no reverence for the treasures taken over from antiquity. The ballet master was satisfied with the most easily accessible, outwardly effective formulas whose extreme meagerness and vulgarity can only hide Fokine's undoubted basic talent from the less perspicacious among the audience.

Moreover, all is not even well as concerns the wonderful invention of Dalcroze who established the method of rhythmic training. Instead of cultivating the new system in an orderly fashion and waiting for results, those associated with the Russian stage hurried to bring the training methods themselves onto the stage for the purpose (cynical or naive, I can't say which) of creating some kind of sensation. The most astonishing thing of all was that even our theoreticians and prophets of rhythmic gymnastics found this artistic debasement, this crude play with the teacher's ideas worthy of approbation. It's impossible, after all, to enhance the reputation of something in which you deeply believe through mistakes like Nijinsky's experiment.

The ballet's second set comprises the greenish obscurity of a cloudy, northern night, a sanctuary on a hilltop, poles topped with skulls rising up. At this point, unexpectedly, an episode filled with fragrant lyricism blossoms forth: girls in red costumes affecting angelic icon gestures, shoulder to shoulder, lead a khorovod. Spreading apart, they search for some kind of mystical path. They select the chosen maiden—the sacrifice—and glorify her with dances. Stooped old men in animal skins surround her in a circle. Hitherto motionless, pale under a white headband, she dances the fatal dance of the doomed. Her knees are drawn together, her toes turned in. A sudden convulsion throws her rigid, contorted body to the side.

She twitches and twists in an ecstatic, angular dance to the fierce beats of the rhythm made deafening by the piercing sounds of the orchestra. And again the chilling comedy of this primitive hysteria disturbs the audience with impressions unheard of in their agonizing grotesquery.

The dance intensifies until the chosen maiden falls lifeless into the arms of the old men.

The nightmare, which, when not replaced by empty mechanics, is performed with rudimentary lyricism and stilted horror, comes to an abrupt end. For the audience it is almost a relief.

Alongside Igor Stravinsky's Cyclopean poem, Claude Debussy's ballet *Jeux* is captivating in its ethereal web of slithering harmonies. Its twitching rhythms are elastic and flexible. Here the ballet master created something very interesting indeed.

Bakst's decor depicts a garden: bright green masses of rather "poster paint" trees, round flower beds, a flat, yellow barrier of rectangular buildings of some kind in the back, an electric street light shining. Two girls and a youth wearing athletic outfits combine movements and poses in a complex but vague love game.

Here Nijinsky moves away even more decisively than Fokine from traditional ideas of the essence of dance. Fokine, leaning toward eclecticism and compromise, tries to justify dance by giving it an emotional base, and an obvious one at that. Nijinsky breaks up the organic unity of dance, chopping it up into a series of separate movements and pauses united only by the unbroken musical accompaniment.

Fokine does not understand the mechanical or aesthetic significance of *tourner le talon* and rejects it in favor of the legs' natural movement. Playing with plastic paradoxes, Nijinsky places the dancers' legs with toes together and heels turned out.

He obtains the movement's plastic form on geometric schematization. All the dancer's poses and movements could be reproduced graphically using straight lines. Both girls have straight, unbent knees, straight torsos, elbows and hands bent at right angles. They move about the stage facing the audience in a precise skip on *demi-pointe*. The only free movement is a wide leap over a flower bed—a welcome interruption of the tension that burdens the audience.

The symbolism of the choppy, angular movements is not clear; the events on stage, almost incomprehensible and lacking nuances, seem overlong despite their actual brevity.

Of course *Jeux* is also a failure. The public rejected it. But in this ballet, in its stiff, poor and contrived form, one discerns a genuine novelty of conception which, perhaps, is not completely futile.

Thus in these sport "jerseys" with ball and racket—traditional tennis emblems—in the impersonal architectural background, some elements of contemporary life are embodied in naive and prosaic symbols. And in the breaks and groupings of tense bodies one clearly senses some sort of contact with the newest trends in painting which strive toward depth and synthesis by way of geometrical simplification—if only in the picturesque parallelism of the Swiss master Ferdinand Hodler.

In Nijinsky's compositions there is some of this significant abstraction. His conception is not banal, but his approach to it lacks depth, creative imagination and conviction.

II
DAPHNIS AND CHLOË, LA TRAGÉDIE DE SALOMÉ, L'APRÈS-MIDI D'UN FAUNE

The Russian performances in Paris came to an end and their exceptional material success can be defined to the same degree as their artistic downfall.

The reasons for this downfall are completely obvious.

With Fokine's departure the troupe lacked a ballet master and had to make do without him; it never did have a *régisseur.* In addition, the permanent corps of performers making up Diaghilev's troupe bears the honorable title "Ballets Russes" only by virtue of the tradition of previous seasons. It is just their trademark. The performers are mostly Polish. English dancers, who received their training in variety theaters, are fortunately distinguished by an innate sense of rhythm. The few Russian performers dissolve willy-nilly into the random crowd of figurants who are French.

No one knows how to do a "Russian" dance in Benois' and Stravinsky's *Petrushka.* (Even some of the members of the Muscovite chorus in *Khovanshchina* do better.) The crowd stamps helplessly and dismally on stage, Nijinsky as *Petrushka*—an inspired image of tragic grotesquery—is almost as brilliant as before and Karsavina as the Ballerina is pleasant too—mechanical doll-like and affected as she is by nature on the stage. Next to them, the Moor is very poor.

The spontaneous, rhythmic dance of Sophia Fedorova blazes up in a flexible, flickering flame in some episodes of *Sheherazade* and *Igor.* Among the *danseurs,* who have come by chance to our notice, there is genuine, distinctive talent.

But these are all details. The point is the "Ballets Russes" is totally lacking in definite, principled artistic intentions. Moving along the path of least resistance, it reaps the golden fruit of past triumphs. Now its only concern is self-preservation. Its new productions are conditioned solely by a relentless demand for novelty. And therefore any and every chance idea that might occur to the ballet master seems desirable and even lifesaving. Fokine's decorative exoticism and dramatic temperament were used up and replaced by Nijinsky's archaic toys and rhythmic mechanics. The enterprise, obedient to tangential impulses, has no organic life or continuity.

An index of this impoverishment was the revival of *Daphnis and Chloë* (with Bakst's decor and costumes) which was staged *à la Fokine.*

What are we to make of this work?

A year ago Fokine realized the production in only three days' feverish work. And now this rough draft has been revived by Nijinsky on the basis of the performers' more or less precise recollections. But because some of them were absent, the new ballet master had to include some newly-invented scenes. To this end he repeated some motifs from his *Faune.*

I could, of course, speak of Maurice Ravel's beautiful score, or of the tremendous impression made by the hidden choruses sounding from the depths of the stage. I could tell the story of the ballet one more time—but none of this would make up for the crudeness and meagerness of the choreographic conception.

Where is the intimate charm of this mysterious poem, the fragrant flower of Hellenic romanticism?

Most of all this intimate quality is lacking in Bakst's decors and costumes. He has replaced the pale marble Hellas of academic tradition with a harsh, motley, polychromatic style. Historically he is correct, of course. The kaleidoscopic juxtaposition of pure tones and the absence of shading sometimes produces very harsh color harmonies. But the red slopes of the cliffs in the second scene do make a strong impression.

The dances and gestures in *Daphnis?* To a great extent they are the repetitions of *Narcisse* by Bakst and Tcherepnine. There is the same dilettante eclecticism, the same superficial museum quality of the Duncan-Fokine style, but as if in the decadent stage.

These dancing Hellenes, barefoot or in sandals, throwing their knees up high, sauntering around in pairs or forming sculptural groups and processions in simulation of ritual mime, are intolerable, like any vulgarization of great art and almost inscrutable sacred objects.

Some exhilaration was introduced by the pirates' boisterous Pyrrhic Dance which, by the way, was not at all unlike a reflection of *Prince Igor.*

But the action is dragged out in a long, boring way. The fashionable falsification of antiquity has been used up, exhausted and wrung out completely.

The soft, sensitive bucolic charms of the poem's episodes are realized with prosaic concreteness, without nuances or depth. Their scenic transformation, not justified by any personal interpretation, is turned into a superfluous, contrived theatrical fakery. There is no lyricism, no effort and, mainly, no art.

Such dance paraphrases can be put together by the dozen.

Now we must turn to Boris Romanov's *La Tragédie de Salomé.* This is no easy task. The inconsistent and amorphous qualities of the choreographic conception impede a clear-cut definition. I did not read Robert d'Humières' program. Apparently he interprets the Salomé legend on a symbolic level, ignoring its concrete episodes and literary traditions. It is a poem of ecstatic passion, arrogance and horror.

The ballet's music was composed by Florent Schmitt, one of the less conspicuous and personal representatives of French musical impressionism. The score's shortcoming is the extreme disproportion of its parts. All its themes are worked out in the excessively long prelude and the very short ballet proper seems a repetition and intensification through movement of the overture's motifs. The heady harmonies of Rimsky-Korsakov and Mussorgsky are circumspectly and diffidently applied by the composer. The women's humming choruses are beautiful and reminiscent of Debussy's irresistible *Sirènes.*

The decors dreamed up and executed by Sudeikin outside the confines of any definite style seemed to lack genuine élan. Many have insisted that the influence of Aubrey Beardsley on them is obvious, but this is hardly justified. We see instead the orange and indigo enamels of the East and Vrubel's faceted amethysts. The influence of the English graphic artist is confined to certain details such as Salomé's lovely, low mitre. For Beardsley is distinguished by an exceptional severity, complexity and precision of linear construction, bringing to mind the fragility of an arabesque, flexible yet strong as steel.

Sudeikin, however, is a colorist and by no means an ordinary one. He is pleasing in his obvious, though captivating, sugary colors and the precious, sensitive beauty of the pictorial subject, which entirely lacks any structural quality or feeling for distinct, imposing forms. On this occasion he only presented a series of ingratiatingly attractive details. Thus, Salomé's entrance is magnificent. She comes down from on high at the back of the stage and her endless mantles trail behind her down the steps of the terrace. The Empress' bare knee is delicately painted by the artist. Nevertheless, this ballet demanded from the designer a greater and more genuine pathos of picturesque suffering.

Romanov's choreography seemed insufficiently defined in both style and intention. It went directly back to Fokine in the form of the movements, but an attempt to re-establish the decorative symmetry of the dancing groups could be observed, a symmetry which in its full measure is characteristic of classical ballet.

We remain unmoved by the expressive content of Salomé's restless, mosaic-like dance. Perhaps it is because there is no trace of tragic suffering in Karsavina's fussy exertions.

La Tragédie de Salomé called forth neither protest nor enthusiastic approval. It is only a sketch.

The revival of Debussy's and Nijinsky's *Faune* was also greeted quietly. I must admit this archaeological experiment seemed insignificant to me.

The hill upon which the Faun rests is parallel to the footlights and drawn up close to them. Only the narrow proscenium remains free and on it there appear nymphs in the typical positions of the dancing figures in ancient vase painting; the audience sees them only in profile. Their movements are confined to the conventional painting formulas of the Greek potters. This creates the rather lapidary and impressive quality of archaic figures.

All the same, the figures of living dancers simulating two-dimensional vase painting create an absurdly weighted-down impression. It is also an unartistic idea to stretch along the footlights the figures that decorate the circumference of a vase in a living wreath, as if they were traced from an archaeology textbook. In addition, Debussy's sonic web is interrupted throughout by the sharp corners of the dance line.

The concentrated and intensive strength of some of Nijinsky's movements as the Faun provide the only animated aspect of this flaccid production.

Our ballet is now experiencing an important period of vacillation and intense experimentation. In order to embody the new content, the emerging forms must experience a rebirth, the nature of which has not yet taken shape.

What is clear is that the fate of Diaghilev's ballet venture (perhaps the most important private venture in the West) is no longer tied to that of the Russian choreographic stage by any solid link.

CHAPTER FIVE

The New Ballet
Versus the Old

W H E N about two years ago the wish arose in me to explain the
artistic basis of the new trends evident in the "Ballets Russes," my
attempt, which appeared as an article entitled "On the New Ballet"
(*Apollon,* No. 8–9, 1911)*, met with great difficulties which have
now been only partly surmounted.

First of all, these new trends which, for the sake of convenience, I
will take the liberty of calling by the collective name "Fokine ballet," have been produced almost exclusively during foreign tours—
our choreography's distinctive "Secession."[1] These unusual circumstances forced me to carry out what I see as the essentially
ungrateful task of describing these celebrated performances. For

_____

*The present chapter was originally a paper delivered at a meeting of a theatrical
circle and later published.

what could be more inadequate than a verbal transcription of visual and musical impressions? Now, however, the recent "Fokine Month" on our own stage has to a great degree broadened our local connoisseurs' field of vision, as it revealed—like the *Orpheus* ballet—the nature of the young innovator's aspirations and the extent of his achievements.

On the other hand, an even more serious drawback became apparent. There were no suitable methods nor ready-made techniques for describing or evaluating the form and content of dance. Contemporary ballet aesthetics is still practically virgin soil. In particular, the Russian ballet until recently lacked not only a theoretical foundation, but any ideology at all.

In the work of my respected older colleagues in ballet criticism, to which I turned with greedy (if I may put it so) curiosity, I found only a day-by-day chronicle and a sometimes imprecise account of Russian ballet history, along with a quantity of individual evaluations. The only question treated with particular passion or breadth turned out to be that of the advantages and disadvantages of different national ballet schools (Italian, French, Russian) seen through their most famous ballerinas.

Thus, left to rely on my own imagination and conjectures, I perhaps did not always find a precise formulation for my assumptions about the essence of ballet, and often had to resort to terminology not endemic to the subject.

Yet, despite the fragmentary nature of my endeavor and the generally ill-disposed attitude toward it on the part of certain entrenched interests, the majority of my theses and even my individual opinions were accepted not only by like-minded people, but even by my opponents.

Fortunately, ballet thought—which had been on such a rudimentary and ineffectual level—has become very animated during the past year. It is still difficult to gauge the consequences of this obvious growth of interest in ballet or the heightening of debate which has been stirred by Volynsky's reviews in *Birzhevye Vedomosti*. It is true he has yet to present an orderly system of classical dance, though the precious elements of such a system may nevertheless be found in his series of articles.

Finally, propaganda for Jaques-Dalcroze's system of rhythmic training prompted Prince Sergei Volkonsky to make a revolutionary reappraisal of all theatrical values, including those concerning the ballet.*

I will have to confront this re-evaluation especially seriously, because at the basis of Prince Volkonsky's critique lies a rather negative view of the basic positions stated in my article.

True, in the heat of polemical onslaught Prince Volkonsky gets things a bit mixed up at times and interprets my words in a rather arbitrary fashion, but this, in my opinion, does not diminish the substance of his objections in the least.

I must admit the title of this chapter is somewhat paradoxical. Speaking about the *new* and the *old* ballet, I seem to be establishing a duality that in reality does not exist. There can be—and who can doubt it?—countless forms of *theatrical dance*, but there is only one *ballet*, and its evolution flows within the close confines of a single artistic principle: classical dance. It would not be too much to assert that classical dance is the only authentic artistic *tradition* we have, the single example of organic *style* in the contemporary Russian theater.

We shall return to an appreciation of this style's extraordinary vitality, but will meanwhile take up the dubious premise about the obsolescence of classical forms or their incompatibility with modern aesthetic criteria, and we shall systematically survey the ways and means which are now being used or which will be used to cure our *malade imaginaire.*

I

The providential or else fatal trait of our contemporary culture is that constantly—as we aspire toward either renewal of form or of content—we turn our gaze toward Ancient Greece. The words "that's how the Greeks did it" wield over us an incomparable fascination and conclusiveness.

Of course, brought up as we are on the theory of evolution, we can no longer accept the authority of Ancient Greece as an absolute,

*See his books *Man on the Stage* [*Chelovek na stsene,* St. Petersburg: Apollon, 1912] and especially *Artistic Responses* [*Khudozhestvennye otkliki,* St. Petersburg: Apollon, 1912].

but we accept subordination to it as the categorical imperative of artistic creation. (And I willingly admit, by the way, that for myself no less than for others, Greece provides an extraordinarily inspiring example.) It is not without reason that all the modern innovators in dance appeal to Greece: Isadora Duncan dancing in front of a photographer in the empty *orchestra* of the Amphitheater of Dionysus and studying ancient relics in museums; the Russian ballet master [Fokine] who created *Eunice,* the Bacchanale series, *Narcisse, Daphnis and Chloë,* the dances of *Orpheus.* Only recently an honorable pedagogue referred to the example of antiquity in his apologia for Jaques-Dalcroze's "rhythmic *orcheisthai.*"

Finally, the work of the newest ballet composers—Ravel, Roger-Ducasse, Tcherepnine, Steinberg and even the ultra-nationalistic Liadov (his *Dance of the Amazon)*—incorporates ancient motifs.

Meanwhile, nothing could be more paradoxical or arbitrary than the usual opposition of classical dance to ancient *orchestic* dance.

The countless attempts that have been made during the past three centuries at recreating ancient dance on the basis of literary sources have been nothing but futile. Only Maurice Emmanuel, in his remarkable book on Ancient Greek dance, succeeded—by comparing over 600 depictions of dance on vases and reliefs with photographic records of modern ballet movements—in creating a precise, reliable picture of these Greek *orcheisthai* which we find so enigmatic.

A few examples will suffice to establish the kinship between classical ballet and ancient *orcheisthai* as well as to dispel a few notorious prejudices about the latter.

I shall present only a brief list so as to avoid the pedantry of complicated terminology.

There is a whole series of movements and *pas* common to both classical ballet and ancient *orcheisthai* as evidenced by ancient relics. These include: *attitudes* (a position in which the dancer stands on one leg on *demi-pointe* while the other is bent at the knee and extended behind); *battements* (where the moving leg approaches the stationary leg for an instant and is then brought back); *jetés* (jumps on one leg); *balancés* (smooth rocking of the body from side to side); *glissés* (where the toe glides along the ground during a step); *entrechats* or *batterie* (where the legs cross during a jump into the air); and even the famed *fouetté* (where the moving leg describes a line like a whip cracking in the air), regarded by many as a relatively recent invention of Italian virtuosos.

Ancient dance is characterized by many movements *terre à terre* and elevation tempi (such as turns in the air and *cabrioles*) in equal measure.

Some of the movements we have described briefly are performed on the soul of the foot, many on *demi-pointe* and some—contrary to popular opinion—on pointed toe: *pointe*. Ballet adopted this last technique of ancient *orcheisthai* only about a hundred years ago.

The simple-minded notion that "natural" bare feet were one of the requisites in ancient dance is primarily founded on the convention of illustration in the plastic arts. The usual footwear of Greek dancers, the thick-soled *krepides*, seems to correspond to our ballet slipper.

The gravitation toward complete nudity or the mandatory half-length tunic is nothing more than the invention of modern Hellenism. Ancient dance loved the complicated play of drapery.

At the basis of ballet's mechanical structure lies the "opposition" principle, formulated originally by Noverre and developed by Carlo Blasis and later Delsarte. It is the principle of cross-associating opposite parts of the body (such as the right arm and left leg or vice versa) in order to achieve the utmost stability and harmony. This principle is repeatedly confirmed in monuments of ancient *orcheisthai*.

This abbreviated list of facts establishes not only a certain analogy between contemporary ballet technique and ancient dance skills, but an organic relatedness as well.

Greek dance was not, as many are inclined to believe, a modification of ordinary movement. It demanded conscious and complex efforts. As with any art, it had artifice as an inherent characteristic.

A sharp boundary between ballet and ancient dance is the completely different role of the *arms*. Though, of course, in movements where the arm and leg positions are mechanically dependent on each other by the "opposition" principle, this difference is not evident.

In the other cases the position of the arms in ballet is governed by considerations of beauty and unity of line, by fixed, decorative formulas. Thus, the position of the hand is dependent on that of the whole arm and even the fingers are subordinated to this stable combination. Our ballet is rich in expressive pantomime which, however, only *alternates* with dance and does not destroy its formal unity.

Ancient dance is dichotomous. The legs dance, the arms speak, the *orchest* is also a *keirosoph.* The hand's decorative position gives way to an eloquent gesture. This gesture should be able to "express everything" and in the "clearest possible way."

The means for the hands' expressiveness have been developed to the extreme; the free hand acted "alone," each finger could play an independent role. One of the elements of hand speech—keironomy—was finger language or dactylology.

Thus, the Greeks combined movements of the arms and legs, dance and pantomime into one whole, while ballet is circumscribed within specific artistic formulas and alternates mechanically with pantomime.

One of the aspects of modern ballet (and salon) dance which, perhaps, dates from around the time of the Renaissance, is the "partnered" dance. The ballerina performs a whole series of movements with the support of the cavalier, and in the majority of these positions the dancing pair obeys the law of "oppositions."

Partnered dances are found in ancient *orcheisthai* as well, though invariably governed by two principles: the dancers' movements are never identical and are not even similar; the dancers never (hardly ever*) touch each other or interlace arms. The dancers often face each other and carry on a mimed dialogue. The purely mechanical function of supporting the ballerina was unknown to the Greek *danseur.*

To an even greater degree all this could be related to "mass" dance, the ensemble of the *corps de ballet.*

The ballet ensemble, in its most perfect form (as preserved for us by Marius Petipa), is entirely based on the aesthetic principle of "unity within diversity." The dance of the *corps de ballet* is made up of harmonious movements of a group of dancers—movements which are not only identical in form and similarly directed, but which also coincide in time. The *danseuses* are usually arranged in rows forming a right angle. The geometric structure increases the unity and impressiveness of the mass movement. In her variations the soloist contrasts with this unified background. Another frequent device is arranging the *corps de ballet* in two rows along the sides of the stage such that they accompany the ballerina or a group of soloists with even, uniform body positions. The path of their dance

---

*Pompeian dancers are an exception.

outlines geometric figures and precisely straight lines on the floor.

According to Emmanuel, ancient *orcheisthai* hardly knew such group unity and symmetry.

Such is the correlation between ancient dance and classical ballet in its most general features. Ballet technique is a complex system of artificial movement, specified down to the most minute details, which developed over the course of two centuries. It restricts the amplitude of movements by precise limitations governed by a particular internal logic, and it moves toward the plane of pure form, away from pantomime's concrete emotions. Its mechanical and decorative canon is unshakable; its development flows within the confines of a single tradition.

Ancient *orcheisthai* was not characterized by such totality. The laws of the dance were expressed less strongly; geometrically correct mass arrangement was unknown to *orcheisthai.* Ancient dance, in the narrow sense of the word, seems to have created a gymnastic and rhythmic foundation for pantomime, whereas ballet is a *specific* dance whose ideal content is expressed in an animate, variable and beautiful *line.*

Here I only want to emphasize that many of ballet's essential, formal characteristics—so zealously sought after by our reformers and restorers—have already been *given* and harmonically developed in so-called "classical" dance, the soul of contemporary ballet. To persecute ballet in the name of antiquity is a blatant misconception.

Of course everyone is free to understand the word "classical" in his own way, though *objectively* it corresponds to the forms that make up the heart of the old ballet.

However, Emmanuel's book embraces only the purely dance and gymnastic aspects of ancient *orcheisthai;* its mimetic, expressive side—which is so very important—is not examined.

What was it like? Was it really a free improvisation of the stereotypically-exuberant Hellene, an immediate expression of his sensibility—some kind of choreographic impressionism? For this is just how some of our propagandists imagine ancient dance.

That this was not the case we learn first of all from literature. Now I admit I am a very mediocre humanist and a totally unexacting archaeologist; furthermore, the texts that have survived (they began to be collected as long ago as the sixteenth century) are either fragmentary or late, noncritical compilations. The only real piece of evidence from the classical era, the treatise on dance by Aristoxenus, the famous theoretician of rhythm, has been lost.* Finally, the precise meanings of Greek *orcheisthai* terminology have yet to be established.

Still and all, we can affirm with complete confidence that no aspect of Greek *orcheisthai* was left to chance or to the dancer's disorderly psychological impulses or moods. The movements and gestures were obviously governed strictly by a canon as immutable as that of a ceremonial rite. Like all Greek theater, it was a particular, hieratic language of forms, perhaps not always comprehensible to the uninitiated. It was not for nothing that Athenaeus—the encyclopedist of the Roman era—in his pithy manual *Deipnosophistae [Banquet of the Sophists]* glorifies the upright Marathonian Aeschylus for being the inventor of some new dance forms and for being a great tragic poet in equal measure.

And what is the method of reconstructing antiquity to which our Neo-Hellenes appeal, in waging war against the old ballet's reputed *pseudo-classicism?* First of all, it goes without saying, they emancipate individuality from strict form (though this preliminary reform is only a variation of the typical Russian revolt of content against form), and then they borrow from antiquity.

The latter technique is simplified to the extreme: in any old album (or, who knows, having carefully gone through a whole pile of albums) the ballet master finds a picture illustrating any single moment of Greek dance. Scrutinizing the movement, he imagines it as the basis of a completely arbitrary choreographic construction. In the same way they used to deal, for example, with Ancient Egypt. They would find a drawing, let's say—in a little primer or a thick *ouvrage* (like Perrot or Chipiez)—depicting dancers performing to musical accompaniment. Their movements are immediately translated into some kind of "Nubian" dance (Fokine's *Eunice*), and right there on stage, in the pose shown in the drawing, Nubian dancers circle around each other. Meanwhile, any careful examination of the drawing would reveal that each dancer circles, so to speak, around his or her own axis (a typical Eastern movement) and not around other dancers.

Or else the ballet master arranges the *corps de ballet* like a bas relief at the very footlights and parallel to them *(Egyptian Nights),* against the three-dimensional stage and decor which extend the per-

---

*Lucian's famous dialogue deals almost exclusively with Roman pantomime.

spective. Thus, the two-dimensional decoration lacks the most important thing of all: the plane it is supposed to adorn.

This is only a sample of the superficial interpretations—so arbitrary and fragmentary, so illogical and incoherent—that endeavor to create for the audience an illusion of historical accuracy or genuine style by means of isolated, remote similarities to ancient dance.

It is an erroneous and thoughtless tendency to reflect in these "ancient" productions conventions that inhere not only in ancient dance itself, but in the painterly or sculptural interpretation of this dance by Greek artists. Our ballet masters, placing the legs in profile to the body, turning the dancers *en face,* or adding sharp angularity to a *port de bras,* perhaps do introduce a fairly-pungent aroma of archaism or exoticism. But the eccentric "archaeology" displayed in *L'Après-midi d'un faune* by Mallarmé and Debussy—with the nymphs in the order and positions of the famous bronze dancers at the Naples museum—is not only superficial, but downright offensive.

We know far too much about the ancient world for such half-baked zeal to have any value.

I repeat: if the lofty spirit of ancient *orcheisthai* lives anywhere today, even as a distant reflection, it is precisely in the forms of our classical ballet. As for the embodiment of the pseudo-antiquarian spirit in the new ballet, that is to be found in Fokine's countless bacchanales. Unfamiliar with the great eurythmy and order of apollonian dance, the ballet master seeks to embody the subliminal, elemental orgiastic power of Dionysus. But Dionysian ecstasy, as Nietszche understood it and expressed it in Schopenhauer's formulas, is the merging of personality ("leaving oneself") with the World Soul, the Universal Will, the highest form of mystical experience. The orgies of the notorious Bacchanale were of a much more ordinary sort. They were an unbridled or, rather, excited, but in all cases external, sweep of movement and gesture deeply immersed in the erotic. This is not transcending personality, but its triumph over discipline and form. This is not Dionysia, but Saturnalia.

However, I am not reproaching Fokine for his absence of religious pathos, for it is impossible to choreograph a genuine, sacrificial, ecstatic dance other than on the basis of living religious passion.

But are we strong enough to penetrate into the secret of the *faith* from which arose the only Hellenic *cult* we know? Even such an authority on the spiritual life of Ancient Greece as Erwin Rohde was skeptical.

There is no use demanding brilliant psychological insights or philosophical enlightenment of the ballet master. He ought not to create a banal surrogate for religious action with his external, skimpy means. When they attempt to replace the missing psychological basis for their creations (and not only the "ancient" ones) by physical eroticism, this shallow and not always pure source dries up with treacherous rapidity.

If the eroticism of *Sheherazade* was exaggerated, that of *Islamay*—analogous in conception—was altogether bombastic.

II

The new ballet, pretentious but poor in content, naturally seeks support in the other arts. Having improved its form and tradition, having shifted its center of gravity from dance to pantomime, the new ballet has tried to borrow its missing significance from painting and music.

Even a year ago, when my article was published, the battle against the dominance of the picturesque over the dynamic essence of choreography was still a dangerous heresy for an author's reputation. Now the wind has begun to blow from the other direction, perhaps even a bit sharply, for every one of us takes great cultural pride in the wonderful set designs of our artists (one need only recall Golovin's *Orpheus* or Anisfeld's *Islamay*). But the principle of the painterly impression of scenic art has finally been shaken. There is a growing inclination toward architectural backgrounds (Reinhardt, Appia), and one senses a general weariness of so-called "productions." Prince Volkonsky's eloquent speech "in defense and glorification" of the *person* on stage was highly symptomatic.

Another concern of the Fokine ballet was to deck itself out in shiny new musical feathers. (Here I am speaking only about Fokine, for Gorsky, the Moscow innovator, is generally indifferent to things musical.) It was a conscientious effort, but one which had already been made by other dilettante innovators: Duncan, Knipper, Fuller, Colonna and, finally, all the "barefooters."

And it's true, who does not feel more akin to Schumann than to Minkus, and who does not favor Chopin—even in his noisy orchestral attire—over Pugni? Ballet has become a pale illustration for a text that needs no illustration. Of course, one *may* interpret the works of great composers in dance or pantomime; it is allowed, and often quite entertaining. But is it *necessary?* Why encroach upon the organic existence of a musical work? After all, the more superficial a balletic interpretation, the more tactful and inoffensive it is. It is no coincidence that many music lovers prefer Fokine's *Carnaval* to his *Sheherazade.*

In connection with the Dalcroze system, here in Russia they have really begun talking about the *révélation* of music through dance. To produce such *exteriorization,* corporeal rhythm should coincide with musical rhythm. One also hears enthusiastic talk about using rhythmic gymnastics to train the deaf and dumb. And truly, one can imagine that the creation of such a dance might permit a deaf and dumb person actually to perceive the music as revealed by the dance. But this perception would inevitably be partial. He would only grasp music's motor, dynamic element, rhythm, naked rhythm, carrying no melody on its undulating waves and deprived of the magnificent vestments of harmony.

But for those of us who *can* hear, is it not simpler to *listen* to music, to immerse ourselves in it directly without resorting to a physical intermediary—that is, the human body?

But let the musicians answer that one. I, for my part, shall return to ballet. The principle of coordinating musical rhythm with dance rhythm is as old as dance itself, and has been practiced continually to a greater or lesser degree. Just so, dance has always proceeded on the same emotional plane as the accompanying music. You not only should not, but you simply *cannot* "danzar la ciaconna sul miserere," as Salvatore Rosa jested in one of his satires. Meanwhile, Prince Volkonsky, in his pursuit of a full, "total" synchronization of dance and music, establishes a rule that is as arbitrary as it is impossible: a single movement for every note. Thus, the model of ideal rhythmic dancing would be the fingers of a pianist in action.

This principle was set forth as long as eighty years ago and was energetically rejected by Blasis. In his commentary on ballet dance, Prince Volkonsky erroneously asserts that in ballet the dance is only appended to the music. On the contrary, the music is appended to the dance. The composer creates a ballet score by coordinating the music with prescribed dance forms, defined rhythmic figures and time units well-tried in choreographic practice. It is agreeable and helpful if the ballet master understands and loves music, but the ballet composer *must* understand dance; only then will the music be, to coin a phrase, *dansant*.

And even Prince Volkonsky asks that *Tanzmusik* have this *dansant* quality, this suitability for dancing. And this is only natural, for music's rhythmic possibilities are infinite whereas body movements, though numerous, are limited.

Even more rigid are the limitations on practicable speed in musical tempo. The aim of choreography, obviously, is not the interpretation of pure musical forms, but the formation of dance music from within the spirit of the dance itself. No doubt to realize their choreographic aims, even the Hellerau students will have to create their own special musical style in accordance with these aims.

Tchaikovsky, Glazunov and Tcherepnine are consciously *dansant*. Stravinsky's *Firebird* is interesting, though not *dansant*, and his *Petrushka*—a wonderful example of musical representationalism—renders the ballet itself superfluous. For contemporary composers, ballet music (like the symphonic poem) is a welcome opportunity for escaping traditional musical forms, though often the idea of someone dancing to their music never even occurs to the listener.

The fact that Minkus and Pugni were also *dansant*, though terrible musicians, proves nothing.

Can Dalcroze's system of rhythmic gymnastics provide ballet with anything that it did not already have on its own? For the Dalcrozians are sometimes even ready to permit the conditional presence of old forms as long as there is a foundation of rhythmic training.

I don't know, and am therefore doubtful.

The obvious victory of these rhythmic gymnastics is the achievement of *automatism* in movement. If, in Kantian categories, Mach and Avenarius found not indispensable modes of thought but well-tried techniques for conserving thought energy, then Dalcroze's achievement proceeds along the same path. The automatism of movement actually does conserve energy, free the mind and make dance easier to perform. In ordinary language we call this result "fluency," such as the fluency of a pianist's fingers or fluency in pronouncing a foreign language.

But contemporary ballet itself possesses this automatism to the highest degree. Its gymnastic foundation and deliberate body culture develop in the dancer—even offstage—an amazing rhythm and ethereality of step and gesture. When performing a *pas* for exercise and without musical accompaniment, the dancer performs each repetition in exactly the same amount of time as the first execution. Moreover, each portion of the *pas*, each intermediate movement coincides in time with the corresponding moments of the first execution. Emmanuel's chrono-photography demonstrated this "isochrony" of movements.

If the history of art is the history of the gradual differentiation of the individual arts, then the dream of their primeval unity (brought to unprecedented heights through the endeavors of Richard Wagner, though not accomplished by him) is mainly an ailment of the contemporary theater. In my view (and not only mine), such fusion, the creation of the *Gesamtkunstwerk* which combines into a single endeavor the highest potentials of all the arts is only possible at a rudimentary stage of their development.

Experience has shown that striving for a synthetic coordination of the arts inevitably leads to the predominance of one and the subordination of the rest. The only surprising thing is that the characteristic feature of the new ballet is the subordination of the main element—dance—to pantomime, and to scenic design with Fokine and to music with Prince Volkonsky.

Classical dance, despite the way it blends so easily with the musical element, has an autonomous existence. It has no need to derive psychological or dynamic impulses from music. It draws directly from the same source that nourishes music as well: the human spirit. (A curious example of natural, non-theatrical dance in which body rhythm is not governed by musical rhythm but is an independent manifestation is Spanish folk dance. It is accompanied by the simple beating out of the rhythm.)

Can we speak of an objective basis for interpreting music? Musical movement can coincide in meter, rhythm, time and "quantity" with body movement. But is "quantity" really the only yardstick; is it really the essence of music?

Gluck's *Orpheus* was performed at the summer *Festspeile* in Hellerau. I was not able to attend and thus read Prince Volkonsky's excellent description with that much greater curiosity. A cursory reading filled me with the spectacle's importance, but on second thought the question arose: where were Gluck and his creation? What could be more arbitrary than such an interpretation? The first German art journal I came across confirmed my assumption: "The spectacle is fresh and promising but . . . not a single point of contact with the *spirit* of Gluck!''

What could Dalcroze have embodied in faces and movements except a series of subjective associations intimated by Gluck's score? How could there be any objectivity here? And how would we know if it were? And, if in fact it were, why is it not obvious to one and all?

III

Prince Volkonsky condemned Fokine's ballet on two counts, with the first of which I concur completely. He accused him of a predominance of the static over the dynamic and of an insufficient coordination between body movement and musical rhythm.

But, on the other hand, this same Prince Volkonsky had occasion to formulate and proclaim a principle particularly important and precious to ballet reformers whether Fokine or Gorsky: Movement is only beautiful when it has purpose and meaning.

Meanwhile, these innovators' greatest concern is in fact the rational justification of dance.

Their job is to find a psychological basis for dance. Movement for the sake of movement—what a waste of time! You must know *why* you are dancing, *for what purpose* you are dancing. Everything must have a reason. That is their motto. Philosophical rationalism has died, but worldly, Philistine rationalism thrives. The teleology that leads to utilitarianism, to the "furnace pot," to the Peredvizhniki[2] lives.

Just recently the last of these epithets was justifiably hurled at the new ballet.

To what emotional experience does the overture to *The Magic Flute* correspond? What is the rational motivation of a Bach fugue? Why do El Greco's saints have elongated extremities?

Because art cannot be broken down into chains of causality.

The apparent irrationality of classical dance, the absence of a firm link between the abstract spirit of a ballet classic and our direct, elementary emotional life prompted our ballet masters (who had savored the vapid green fruits of a semi-cultured state) to distrust dance in general and to embrace pantomime, picturesqueness, genre, archaeology. They are ready to sacrifice everything for the sake of psychological realism, for the sake of the faithful, vivid depiction of affects. They envy the drama where everything is motivated. Their minds seek what is comprehensible, accessible, explicable, demonstrable.

How happy these empty-headed reformers must be at the support of such a cultured writer as Prince Volkonsky who, along with them, inquires: "What does it mean that a person spins like a top?"

Along with the demand for psychological intelligibility, another demand is put forth: "naturalness."

The favorite criterion of the naturalistic school of blessed memory! But in ballet its time has come. When the naturalistic tendency had passed in literature it captured the dramatic theater; having passed through drama as well, it moved on to ballet.

Life is the law of art—thus once again resound the fighting words. But it seems to me that this is debatable. Life is the material of art, but can material (be it marble or the human body) really carry within itself creative laws? "The highest goal of architecture," affirms Reinach in his very popular book on art, "is transcending the material's suggestions."

From the elements of nature the artist creates a new reality. He is given concrete facts in order to combine them into an imaginary existence; he is capable, according to Goethe, of realizing the imaginary. What are the limits of the natural? And where is that "natural" man to whom Rousseau's newest followers appeal?

If I have affirmed (as I have been accused) in my article that "rising on *pointe* the ballerina is released from natural movement," (which I cannot take back), by "natural" I meant ordinary, mechanical, involuntary movement.

In so doing I provided the keepers of artistic morals with as little basis for taking me to task as if I had said, "Having begun to sing, the singer is released from natural speech."

Everyone would have understood me, and no one would have condemned me.

There are no absolute standards of beauty in art. The value of my hypotheses (though they are commonplace in modern artistic thought) is inevitably relative. But the standard of naturalness is positively groundless, perished long ago, and moreover is devoid of definite content.

It seems I have enumerated all the methods used for improving and curing the ballet: cures by antiquity, painting, music, rationalism, psychology, naturalness. The efforts and labors of our newest ballet masters have been swallowed up by endeavors to save ballet from the constraints of classical dance.

Prince Volkonsky has occupied a special position in the ballet debate. Judging the art from the point of view of naturalness, he chose a *non-ballet* point of view (Prince Volkonsky's own expression) for judging ballet. This method speaks for itself.

Ardently convinced of a coming renewal of the art which will bring with it *der alleinseligmachende Rhythmus* and its prophet, Dalcroze, he sentenced ballet to a grandiose auto-da-fé in his last book in order to clear the way for a new edifice.

Though we place great expectations in Dalcroze's venture—expectations that even all these inflated messianic prophesies about a future golden age cannot shake—we still cannot follow Prince Volkonsky in this "act of the faith," and return once again to the ballet, this time to the so zealously-persecuted *classical* ballet.

I won't dispute that classical ballet's aesthetic essence is difficult to define. Even the ancient philosopher admitted that in general "it is difficult to define the beautiful."

We can describe all the technical and gymnastic aspects of classical dance, but finding a psychological equivalent for each of its movements is an impossible as well as unnecessary task. Of course classical dance is not conditioned by any external force. It has its own immanent law, its own internal logic, whose every infringement is perceived by the audience as an infringement on the artistic impression.

One of the laws of classical dance is aplomb, the search for steady equilibrium. "A simple, grim necessity that gives the ballerina a point of rest," Prince Volkonsky scornfully characterizes the ballet slipper. The necessity is neither simple nor grim.

Is not all architecture, for example, based on such grim necessities? What is a contraforce if not a force balancing the pressure of an arch? What is a Doric colonnade if not a system of columns supporting the equilibrium of the crossbeam? What does the contraforce express? What experiences do these columns describe? And who is to say that the Temple of Neptune does not express the human soul?

Classical dance is in many ways analogous to architecture insofar as movement may be compared to immobility. Like architecture, it is the result of spatial, geometric thought; it is *Raumkunst* as the Germans call architecture.

It abstracts its noble instrument—the human body—into building units. The skeleton of dance is the same as a temple plan: the line. Classical dance gravitates toward pure, unbroken lines. This is why it does not need the sculptural peculiarities of the parts of the body that break up this linearity. An example would be how the ballerina's leg, in an *attitude* on toe (and here I particularly mean the ballerina and not the *danseur* in general, for movement on toe is her special domain), with an arched instep and pointed toes creates a vertical line of amazing purity. Here the leg's shape, subordinated to the single movement of the whole body, loses its individual characteristics and becomes stylized, generalized.

What my critic, Prince Volkonsky, did not take into consideration in his admiration of the leg itself, was the structural and linear unity of the entire dancing figure. The fact that he prefers movement on *demi-pointe* to that on *pointe* is a matter of personal taste. And I readily admit perhaps the Ancient Greeks shared this preference.

Among Prince Volkonsky's virtues, along with his beguiling style and great enthusiasm, is a multitude of ready-made theories "for any eventuality." Can an opera singer's "willful" impulses be reconciled with the demands of rhythm? He limits his individual rights in the name of an overriding principle, the rhythm. Must the hateful ballet slipper be destroyed? He defends the individuality of each toe.

But one cannot maintain that any generalization is contrary to art, that the process of artistic creation is exclusively a process of individualization! That is, you can maintain it, of course, but you can also maintain the opposite.

Does the artist not move from the individual to the general, casting off the inessential characteristics along the way? Is artistic creation really not the uninterrupted deformation of reality? Does the artist's path really not lead him from the concrete to the symbolic?

Who will raise his hand against generalization, that is, according to Prince Volkonsky, against the "stencil and routine" and so forth of Egyptian sculpture, the Ravenna mosaics, the Siena frescoes? Does Phidias really not generalize in the Panathenaic frieze? No, the passionate protest against generalizing is just as much a double-edged blade as the demand for naturalness.

In my "incriminating" article (which is, as I said, extremely fragmentary), I neglected to mention one other principle of classical dance: *jambes en dehors*. Here again is "unnaturalness caused by the grim necessity" of aplomb! The result of this quality (which the dancers develop during their years of gymnastic training) is not only an increased freedom and stability of movement, but also a greater amplitude of movement. (An example is the angle formed by the moving and stationary leg which may be *développé*-ed to a right angle.) Another result is the multiplanar quality of the movement which contrasts to a movement performed in a single plane.

Noverre was a staunch supporter of turned-out legs, as was Carlo Blasis after him and Volynsky in our own day.*

Such a leg position is, of course, not a characteristic of the natural person. But theatrical dance is not the impulsive, irregular dance of a primitive savage! More than anything else, ballet is an artificial and not a natural dance.

During the *Ancien Régime,* with its unsurpassed formal culture, theatrical dance still partly coincided with court and salon dance from which it broke only at the end of the century. When the fashion of choreographic training declined, not only dance but its basic positions became impractical for the non-dancer. This transition is extremely well described in Oskar Bie's book about dance.

When dance became the exclusive property of professional artists, it gained in artificiality and, along with that, in spirituality. The idealistic cult of *pointe* and elevation, which serves as the basis of modern ballet form, only arose at the beginning of the nineteenth century. Even Noverre was not yet familiar with revolving movements on toe or protracted equilibrium in *attitudes en pointe.*

The contemporary crisis in classical dance is not a new ailment for ballet; it is periodically repeated. Its unchanging symptom is the predominance of pantomime.

In the middle of the eighteenth century ballet suffered a rationalistic crisis, at the beginning of the nineteenth, a Romantic one. Both threatened classical dance, but from both it emerged enriched, and the evolution of its technique was uninterrupted. The centuries through which ballet has passed have left their mark on its scenic construction. The Romantic libretto of the 1830s continues to reign even now, and the legacy of the affected Rococo and even the mag-

---

*Our innovators erroneously think turned-out legs to be an innovation of the modern Italian school, while Taglioni's style is the transcendence of the technique. It was Taglioni herself who laid the foundation for the virtuoso style of women's dance.

nificent allegory of the French Baroque break through this Romantic outer layer. We can love these souvenirs of the past—light as pollen on a butterfly's wings—but the living soul of ballet lies not in this sweet folly, in this sentimental, ironic stylization.*

Now ballet is experiencing a third crisis, and I don't know if it will be as fruitful as the first two. I am only sure the phoenix of classical dance will rise from the ashes. And with it will combine more significant and modern theatrical ideas. It will fly in new and picturesque plumage. Everything that is accidental, temporary, inessential, everything that darkens its existence will painlessly fall away.

Classical dance is a world of countless possibilities. And it is just such conditions of artificial equilibrium that enhance its wealth. It is true the number of its basic forms is finite, as is the number of basic colors on an artist's palette, but the number of possible shades and combinations is greater than we can imagine. It is only to vision that lacks culture, that knows nothing of fine distinctions, that ballet will seem monotonous, just as the poet's measured speech seems monotonous to the untrained ear.

It seems to me on the whole the old ballet suffers from another, extremely dangerous evil: an unreconciled duality, the antinomy between the psychological qualities of pantomime and the ideal nature of classical dance. Resolving this contradiction (and the Greeks managed) is the task of the near future.

And in this I join ranks with our reformers. But, while they sacrificed dance to pantomime with the greatest of ease, I would have been more inclined to cleanse the lofty sphere of artistic dance of the primitive realism and cheap psychology of its vaunted pantomimes.

But it is about time we asked, what have they accomplished? What new choreographic treasures have they created? I don't dispute their undeniable talent, but what has been their contribution? Even the fans of their innovations reject Fokine's first ballets as obsolete (this is in the space of two to three years) and others maintain that he has long since begun to repeat himself. It seems they are both right. Fokine created the Polovetsian Dances from *Prince Igor,* which endure.

---

*Such as Volkonsky's *Powdered Marquise.*

No, the course of the ballet of the future will move on another psychological plane. What will it be like? At this point I don't think we can hazard a guess.

Let no one reproach me for not having proved the advantages of the classical ballet. Proof is easy only when the whole issue consists of words.

Thus, my endeavor should not be taken as an apologia. I only wished to explain—without any balletomanic conceit—my own point of view, and to attempt to interpret certain phenomena, remove some prejudices (such as the philistine cult of naturalness) and, mainly, pose a series of questions with an acuity and precision that demand either agreement with my arguments or substantive objection to them.

If I have achieved this, the goal of this article has been fulfilled.

Notes to Chapter Five

1. A reference to the independent exhibitions held in Berlin, Munich and Vienna during the last decade of the nineteenth century.
2. The *Peredvizhniki* were a group of artists who broke from the Academy in 1863 as a reaction against the prevailing trends of neoclassicism. They based their artistic principles on realism and the life of the common people. Supported by Vladimir Stasov and Pavel Tretyakov, they established the Association of Traveling Art Exhibitions in 1870. See: Elizabeth Valkenier, *Russian Realist Art* (Ann Arbor: Ardis, 1977).

CHAPTER SIX

Reviews and Episodes

I
ABOUT *DANSEURS*

T H E last act of *Raymonda,* which was recently performed on the
Russian stage, contained, as usual, the *grand pas hongrois,* one of
the most complicated and magnificent creations of the aged Marius
Petipa's decorative and rhythmic genius. This choreographic poem,
conceived on an unusually broad scale, includes the unique "variation for four *danseurs.*" It is a difficult test for the performers (on
this occasion Messieurs Andrianov, Leontiev, Semenov and Anatole Obukhov) who, if not brilliantly, emerged at least honorably.

The structure of the finale is especially impressive. After a general pause, the four performers join in a dance, entering one after

the other, like the voices of a fugue (if such a comparison be permitted for such a short choreographic figure).

But beyond the purely technical significance and quality of these performances, one other factor ought to have lent them the aura of sensation. For except in Russia, such problems have not been tackled by any ballet troupe in the world for several decades now.

It is not without reason that the *danseur* has been virtually neglected by contemporary balletomanes, critics and even historians of the ballet. Ballet is taken by so many to be simply an emanation in movement of the feminine principle, its secret emotional essence—wherein visually perceived lines and colors are permeated with a refined—almost dematerialized—sexual appeal. By others (chiefly through having seen the seraphic revelations of the "Christian dancer," Marie Taglioni), it is taken to be one of the embodiments of the Eternal Feminine whose charms transcend the merely sensual, that is to say, as an allegory, a code.

In any event, the Romantic era of ballet, which lay the foundations for the predominance of the ballerina over the ensemble, reduced the role of the *danseur* to a purely auxiliary one. While the ballerina executes technical movements on *pointe,* the *danseur* performs on *demi-pointe.* And, to members of the new bourgeois culture, so efficient, utilitarian and hypocritical en masse, so purely intellectual at their peak, who have allowed the expressive gesture and the rhythmically measured movement to wither—the role of the *danseur* seemed unworthy, frivolous, and even unnatural in the changed social surroundings, like a deviation from the contemporary ideas of "masculinity," a prejudice that remains with us even now. Even Nijinsky's unparalleled success has only partially rectified the artistic and social degradation of the *danseur.*

The fact is that the tradition of the *danseur* ended in the West long ago, as we have shown. Théophile Gautier calls Perrot *l'aérien,* its last representative in France.

And even Perrot (Petipa's predecessor as ballet master here, and the creator of *Faust* and *Esmeralda*), the master of "downhill flights," owed his miraculous technique not to any ballet training, which he never had, but to his professional skill as an acrobat which he acquired in the course of six years' work on the circus stage where he appeared as Pulcinello.

Even fifty years ago the celebrated Copenhagen ballet master, Bournonville in the foreword [sic][1] to his collection of "choreographic exercises," advised *danseurs* "not to fear the injustice of foreign critics who, without regard for talent, reject the *danseur* out of hand."

"Theatrical dance," he added, "which is to say ballet, cannot manage without the participation of men and does not permit female travesties."

However, this last method—travesty—reigns on the French stage. (Here it is only now and then adopted in "character" ensembles.) The role of the *danseur* is, at best, limited to supporting the ballerina.

Perrot is responsible for the exceptional flowering of male dancing which has been one of the enlivening foundations of the Russian stage. Within a short period, masters such as Legat, Nijinsky, Fokine, Andrianov, Mordkin and Valinin have appeared. And, recently, there emerged outstanding younger talents: Vladimiroff, Semenov, Anatole Obukhov. It is no accident that the above mentioned variation from *Raymonda* includes such essential elements of male dance as *entrechats, pirouettes* and turns in the air. The notorious *entrechat* (the etymology is "interlacing—*intrecciata, cabriole*) consists of a single or repeated crossing of the legs during a vertical jump in the air, ending with a fall onto one leg. The number of segments in the broken line drawn in the air by each of the crossing legs gives the *entrechat* its name: *entrechat-quatre, entrechat-six* (the most elegant and especially cultivated by our *danseurs*), and so forth up to *entrechat-quatorze,* a virtuoso tour de force sometimes accomplished by Italian dancers. The greatest difficulty is, naturally, that the multiple movements take place within the short period of falling after the jump.

One of the most important requirements for performing the *entrechat,* besides the strength and elasticity of the extension leg and the muscles which serve as a spring, is the appropriate twist. The legs are crossed at the very ankles while the knees are turned *en dehors* (outward). The waving of the legs forms flickering beams of light which Noverre, by analogy to painting, called "the chiaroscuro of the dance." With knees drawn together, the dancer's legs form an indistinguishable mass, "blurring" his *entrechats.*

The *entrechats* of our *danseurs* are irreproachable, although lacking in virtuoso brilliance. This type of dance is rather unsuitable for Andrianov with his great height. Leontiev, on the other hand, who is small and disproportionately built with his large head, athletic torso and small, muscular legs, achieves in them genuine lightness and grace.

Another principal part of the male dance is the *pirouette.* Gaëtan Vestris, the "dieu de la danse" and the founder of that celebrated ballet dynasty, used *pirouettes* sparingly and circumspectly, forcing the audience to wait for each of them as a rare satisfaction. His son, the brilliant Auguste, was to a great degree obliged by his fame as a revolutionary and eccentric of the dance to perform abundant and diverse *pirouettes.* (The *pirouette*—a device well known to the ancient Greek *danseurs* as well—is a circular twisting of the body in which one leg serves as fulcrum, the impulse giving sweep to the arms.)

The forms and nuances of the *pirouette,* depending on the position of the "free" leg and the direction of the movement, are countless. Our *danseurs* do them primly and without much variety. Their movement is forever, to put it crudely, almost exactly like a corkscrew's. Only occasionally is the *pirouette* used in wide second position where the free leg forms a right angle with the fulcrum leg. Here the great master is the Moscow danseur Tikhomirov who is otherwise heavy and prosaic. It seems to us that such restriction is mistaken.

Carlo Blasis, the Milan ballet master, teacher and theoretician, taught his students to perform *pirouettes* in all positions. In his own time, he would begin *pirouettes* in second position and, after two or three turns, would bend his body into an *arabesque* and conclude the movement in an accelerating tempo. Or else he would *pirouette* with his body stretched out and stooped as far forward as possible— alarming his audience who anticipated his seemingly inevitable fall. Sometimes, finally, he would rotate in what he considered to be the most beautiful of sculptural poses—that of Jean de Bologne's Mercure, caduceus in hand. We may also observe a similar flexibility in Fokine's Polovetsian Dances from *Prince Igor* where the wild archers *pirouette* shaking their weapons. We would prefer such variety to other striking novelties on the order of those used by Legat and Fokine, such as a heavy fall onto one knee after a jump. This we recently saw in several variations performed by Vladimiroff; this *danseur* has gained at last a most precious skill for doing *pirouettes.* His toes have learned at last to grab the floor or "bite" it, as Noverre would say.

From the inexhaustible language of ballet forms I have selected for my extremely schematic exposition merely two examples, two letters of the choreographic alphabet which particularly pertain to the *danseur*.

Perhaps from the sketches for these techniques I have offered the reader can glean an impression of the bare mechanism of the movements discussed here. Perhaps some might even liken a *danseur* performing a *pirouette* to a top. That, of course, would be wrong. A top is activated by a push from without. It is passive—a machine. A *pirouette* is governed by the conscious, concentrated will of the artist who controls each muscular vibration as he throws his body into a picturesque, transporting maelstrom.

Remember Nijinsky's phenomenal jumps! Without obvious preparation, without the deep squat of a *plié,* he would suddenly and lightly soar, as if hovering for an instant in the air, and then come down almost noiselessly.

You can put the most run-of-the-mill *danseur* on a trampoline and it will throw him much higher than Nijinsky, but it would be a mechanical stunt, whereas Nijinsky's jump is a miracle of strength, harmony, self-control and music.

Here the material impulse, the contraction of the muscles, is hidden by the art. Elemental male strength is tamed by the effortless, matchless grace of an ephebe.

We have too long been blind to the beauty and richness of the static and dynamic forms in "classical" ballet. We were too busy and excited with all that is peripheral to dance itself: the costumes, the miming, this or that treatment of the subject, the beautiful image. The actual combination of masses and lines seemed secondary and less interesting to us. Classical ballet seemed monotonous, obsolete; it seemed that we knew it inside out.

Meanwhile, wearied as if by routine, and thirsting for novelty, perhaps we never looked at dance as dance, and never had any conception of the aesthetic value of its complex construction, in a word, never even saw what we were looking at all these decades. It cost us nothing to give up that which we never possessed in our souls to begin with.

I have touched upon male dancing only in its self-sufficient manifestations. Its "applied" role must still be defined.

One tends to speak about the primary function of the *danseur*—supporting the ballerina—with haughty disdain. But actually, what a source of enlivening form is the contact between simultaneous and connected, yet directionally-opposed movements of the dancing couple, the "opposition" between the ballerina and the cavalier! And how his support increases the strength, height and dash of her jump! Are these flights of the ballerina not beautiful when she is carried by the *danseur*—the product of two active forces?

For now I shall ignore the other features of the rich repertoire of male dance: character and mime roles. I only wished to explain by examples that from the voluminous material of "classical" dance (or, if you like, "classy," though you wouldn't call it that) it is possible to extract the elements of that great art of theatrical dance toward which those of us are striving who have grown tired of the psychological trivialization and impoverishment, both in form and content, of the contemporary theater.

II
FOKINE ON THE MARYINSKY STAGE

LES PRÉLUDES

It would appear that never before has the whim of a capricious talent led Fokine into such a blind alley. What vain vagary prompted him to interpret in scenic images Liszt's romantic, pastoral and triumphant tone poem *Les Préludes?*

If ballet is not to be altogether a parasite of others' musical glories, for the scenic treatment of masterpieces of non-theatrical music is by its very nature *excessive,* as is any pleonasm, then such treatment of Liszt's symphonic poem should have been forbidden to any true artist. Had not Liszt already pushed back the ordinary boundaries of musical expression by strengthening the philosophical and psychological sides of his conception almost to the point of palpability?

Is not the obvious goal of all "program" music to express everything—the outer and inner worlds—by musical means alone?

Moreover, Liszt's famous poem is unfolded by means that are not at all choreographic. Its rhythm is almost completely lacking in dance flavor. Is that not why the stage form has turned out so amorphous, scanty and random, so unsuccessfully "dreamed up" by the ballet master to accompany the musical text?

The ballet takes place in a fantastic blossoming paradise (Fiesole or Tahiti?) created by Anisfeld's brush. In the distance, with the transparency of stained glass windows, steep mountain peaks show violet, on brown hills fruit-bearing orange trees loom darkly. But the conventional and idyllic dream of quattrocento masters is framed by lush and fiery tropical vegetation—a bright reminder of the interlacing of exotic motifs in the garden of "The Marriage of Zobeide."

The hero, a swarthy, half-naked youth, carries on a mimed dialogue of love with a pale maiden. Her hair is strewn with green powder (remember Bakst's blue-haired Cleopatra?) and she wears a delicate tunic covered with rare flowers, like a Botticelli nymph.

Nine companions dressed in soft colors (forces of luminous femininity) echo their movements, dividing into three groups like the "three graces" of the Florentine romancer, they join hands in a circle and rise on *demi-pointe* (Duncan's favorite motif) or else, coming out of the circle into a curling line, they move in single file like a display of rhythmic gymnastics.

But the idyll is interrupted by a somber procession of the forces of darkness wrapped from head to toe in long, black cloaks with spots. They emerge from the wings with a rather comically inflated stateliness (the same kind of phantoms appear in the dreams of the Tahitian girls in Gauguin's paintings). In two disorderly crowds, with hysterical and helpless gestures (here a wave of spasmodic laughter ran through the audience) these low beings approach the girls. The youth leaps into their midst and puts them to flight.

The stage fills up again, this time with an even larger swarm of bright beings seized with bellicose rejoicing. But the merciless powers of darkness close in once more, extending across the entire width of the stage, and fiercely and slowly approach the corps, quivering in its joyful dance.

It was in such a spirit of vulgar symbolism that the ballet master cast Liszt's romantic melancholy and heroic pathos.

It befell us to witness in the ballet as well what has already resounded on the dramatic stage: the nightmarish, materialistic and chaotic symbolism of [Leonid Andreyev's] *The Black Masks* and *The Life of Man.*

I don't think the new ballet requires a technical evaluation. It has been liberated from the constraints of form. Its language of movements is childishly impoverished (perhaps intentionally), primitive and mechanical. The symmetrical and aerial motifs of classical dance, naturally, have been banished altogether.

The ballet master has obviously been carried away by a vain wish to rival Dalcroze. In sections dance has been replaced by the beating out of the rhythm with the hands and feet. Energetic stamping corresponds to accented notes and pauses correspond to extended notes. There are even attempts to convey the tempo's acceleration and slowing by an unwitting parody of the "system" so studiously created. But aren't they trying to pull our leg with this pretentious eccentricity?

FRANCESCA DA RIMINI, STENKA RAZIN, EROS

There's no denying that Fokine knows how to captivate and inspire even the most obstinate audience with blandishments of lofty musical beauty, significant subjects, and the charm of names like Dante, Tchaikovsky, Chopin and Glazunov. Even the printed program is richly suggestive, evoking countless associations of the most varied kind. One thinks of the ancient world, the Quattrocento, the mystical Middle Ages, legendary Russian exploits, sultry oriental languor, the torments of Dante's Inferno, the tragedy of prostrate Poland, the romance of a white-columned country estate, idyllic Tuscan glades. You can find anything in this thick network of passions and memories. Even before this Fokine was up to his ears in debts to the painters, composers, librettists and directors who involved him in their attempts to renovate the Russian stage. With each production his debt to the neighboring branches of art grew until they exceeded his means.

Fokine freely draws upon the copious fund of musical masterpieces. Tchaikovsky and Glazunov have now followed Rimsky-Korsakov, Schumann, Liszt and Balakirev (alongside the "exploitation" of Glinka and Mussorgsky). The ballet master willingly reduces the living creation of movement—dance and pantomime—to the level of uninvited additions or idle commentaries to the musical works. He does not proceed from deep creative motivations—personal feeling or inspiration—from which as a rule arise the scenic conception, the character of the gestures and movements, as well as the colors and forms of the musical background. (This would be the path of a genuine master of dance who has a creative imagination and not a "reproductive" one.) On the contrary, Fokine tries to have his quests coincide with the superlative, already completed conceptions of others, that is, to warm himself at another's fire.

To thrust a scenic interpretation onto poor *Francesca* could not have been easier for our insouciant ballet master. Nothing could keep him from his insolent resolution to disgrace Alighieri with his parody. One might say it's "public domain," for if Tchaikovsky's creative experience the Francesca episode hadn't been completely drained within the limits of a symphonic poem, he would have preferred a different, more "adequate" form. Instead of introducing the well known terzets from the fifth canto of the *Inferno* into the score only as an epigraph, he might have created from them a musical drama or cantata. But, considering the complete, wholly-congruent embodiment the composer achieved, to what end is all this earthbound "realization," this fuss in the soul and on the stage, this abbreviated paraphrase of Francesca's lamentable story through a series of illuminations, these dances of Botticelli nymphs, this utilization of Dante's figure as a "framing device" (and anyway, what arrogance and what an affront it is to present Dante himself to the viewer), these contrived, illustrative stunts? What is the point of the careless exploitation of two masterpieces, this attempt to cash in on the literary prestige of a subject which has already attracted so many playwrights, from Silvio Pellico to Averkiev, Crawford to D'Annunzio?

It takes more than just skillful and resourceful stagecraft or thoughtless talent to simply "create" a Francesca. What chaotic pantomime and running around on the stage, what pathetic arm winding and torso bending, what flights on pulley can reproduce the infernal maelstrom that cures the damned "sinners of the flesh" *de qua, di là, de giù, di su,* hither and thither, high and low? How is it the ballet master's hand didn't tremble when he willfully allowed Tchaikovsky's lyrical second theme, in which all the heavenly sweetness of Francesca's confession sounds forth, to become a series of separate episodes and pauses culminating in the scene of the double murder of Paolo and Francesca? How is this infringement on the legend's eternal beauty justified in the name of such "choreographic melodrama"?

The same mechanical synthesis of scenic and musical elements is present in *Stenka Razin,* to Glazunov's music. With the exception of the dancing motifs, the action takes place not "to the music," but as if alongside it—coinciding to it in its rhythm and major accents, but not "emerging" inevitably from it. The action develops from Russian "choreographic folklore" (the dances of the Cossack rebels) and the exotic arm and torso dances (the Persian prisoners). In the first there are many echoes of the Polovetsian Dances from *Prince Igor* and, perhaps, of *Le Coq d'or;* in the second there are flash reminiscences of *Sheherazade* and *Egyptian Nights.* At the basis of the plot is the famous legend of Stenka Razin, who was thrown into his beloved Volga. The interpretation is elementary and crude in its quantity of picturesque and attractive details. Some of the performers are good. In general it is a rather superficial substitute for the genuine national character which is still not to be found on our ballet stage. The whole thing gives the impression of makeshift improvisation.

The third ballet, *Eros,* is just as unacceptable from the musical point of view, but is significant with regard to the evolution of Fokine's style. This composition, about which we must speak in detail since it has been included in the permanent repertoire, marks an attempt by the ballet master at a compromise with classical traditions—on the whole the attempt, like any compromise, is fruitless.

In this ballet, whose dramatic content is taken from Svetlov's story "The Fiesole Angel," the music of Tchaikovsky's *Serenade* is most inappropriately "set to dances."

In a prophetic dream which appears to a young girl, a statue of the ancient Eros, which has miraculously come to life and stepped from its marble pedestal, and a painted figurine of a Tuscan angel, a strange gift from her fiancé, join in battle for her heart: in other words, terrestrial love versus celestial love. Combining reality and magic, in accepted romantic style, the action is set in the pavilion and grounds of a Russian estate in the 1840s. This gives the pretext for a curiously deliberate mixture of styles. The winged god draws the "prim young lady" into the nocturnal dances of his nymph-servants clad in calf-length "Taglioni" tunics. The appearance (unsuccessful to the point of absurdity in terms of staging) of a quattrocento angel with the winding, modern movement breaks the pagan spell. Awakened from the sweetly poignant nightmare, the heroine sees the statue of Eros lying broken on the garden pedestal, and under her pillow she finds the angel doll.

Perhaps indeed it is possible to find the makings of a poetic impression in such a subject—but how hopelessly mechanical the ballet's structure appears in its childlike symbolism!

The fact is that even though Fokine uses the music only as a "backdrop for the mood," he is completely tied to it, and it compelled him to coordinate the changes occurring on stage with the sequence of the themes, tempi and rhythms in the musical accompaniment. Thus, the meeting of the girl and her fiancé and the final, inner revelation are squeezed into a few measures. She even dozes for a moment after their parting. But what can you do? Tchaikovsky's finished musical text cannot be cut up or lengthened!

Our ballet master has once before solved a similar scenic problem in an incomparably more convincing way: *Le Spectre de la Rose,* based on Théophile Gautier's poem and Weber's *Invitation to the Dance.* The ballerina's somnambulistic, involuntary gliding on toe creates the impression of spellbound sleep. In *Eros* the transition from reality to dream is poorly expressed, the forms and movements seem material and tactile.

Even the form of the dance is reduced to the basic devices of the classical school, but in an insincere, contrived, "stylized" interpretation. *Batterie* and the complicated *pirouettes* are employed as if made to order for Kchessinska's virtuosic skill. The elements of the classical adagio, sometimes unusually beautiful and resourceful, are more often masked and distorted by the choreographer. It is as if Fokine, having broken with the strict symmetry of the old school, were attempting to join together disparate fragments of choreographic phrases into a kind of Wagnerian "endless melody." Something of the affected, though very attractive, lyricism of *Chopiniana* made itself felt in the ensemble that forms the basis of the entire scene.

I have extracted only two episodes from my critical diary of a whole five-year span because they seemed suitable for an additional demonstration of already-established positions. For my description of the Paris seasons, the quintessence of the new ballet, renders superfluous any pedantic and petty ennumeration of the experiments which are only remnants of Diaghilev's beginnings. And especially as the fascination of the St. Petersburg experiences with the new ballet has dissipated quite quickly by itself. The legendary prestige of triumphs abroad remains unshakable because it has not been eclipsed.

Is it not enough to set the spell of dilettantism, which has seized the Russian ballet, side by side with the majestic clarity of classical art in order to expose the superficial charms of the dubious novelty? And if, through the chaotic swarm of images that I have evoked of this novelty, the divine countenance of real art has glimmered even for a moment, then the goal of this book has been achieved.

Note to Chapter 6

1. The citation is actually not from the foreword, but from the conclusion of Auguste Bournonville's *Etudes chorégraphiques,* Copenhagen, 1861.

Bibliography

This bibliography does not presume to be complete. André Levinson wrote for such a variety of periodicals—both large and small—in Russia, France, Germany and the United States that the compilation of a comprehensive list is a separate undertaking entirely. Instead, this bibliography serves to indicate the scope of his activity and the volume of his work.

1903

"Anna Pavlova" in *Al'bom Solntse Rossii*, St. Petersburg, 1903, pp. 1–3.
"O Preobrazhenskoi" in *Al'bom Solntse Rossii*, St. Petersburg, 1903, pp. 9–11.
"Tri roli M. F. Kshesinskoi" in *Al'bom Solntse Rossii*, St. Petersburg, 1903, pp. 5–7.

1908

Aksel Gallen: Suzhdenie o kharaktere tvorchestva i proizvedeniakh khudozhnika, St. Petersburg, 1908.

1911

"O novym balete" in *Apollon*, St. Petersburg, 1911, Volume 8, pp. 30–49; Volume 9, pp. 16–29.
"Loi Fuller i eia shkola" in *Apollon*, St. Petersburg, 1911, Volume 9, pp. 65–66.
"Pervyi vykhod g-zhi Pavlovoi; 'Baiaderka' v Mariinskom teatre" in *Apollon*, St. Petersburg, 1911, Volume 13, pp. 202–203 [cited from secondary source].

1912

Eugene Lermans, text by André Levinson, [St. Petersburg,] Khronos, [1912?].

"Novye knigi" in *Apollon,* St. Petersburg, 1912, Volume 1, pp. 73–75.

"Noverr i estetika baleta v XVIII veke" in *Apollon,* St. Petersburg, 1912, Volume 2, pp. 11–35.

1913

"O starom i novom balete" in *Ezhegodnik imperatorskikh teatrov,* 1913, Vyp. 1, pp. 1–20.

"Novye knigi: *Aforizmy*" in *Rech',* St. Petersburg, 28 January 1913, p. 3.

"Don Kikhot" in *Rech',* St. Petersburg, 29 January 1913, p. 5.

"Russkii balet v Parizhe" in *Rech',* St. Petersburg, 3 June 1913, p. 2.

"Pizanella, ili Dushistaia smert' " in *Rech',* St. Petersburg, 8 July 1913, p. 2.

"Balety Nizhinskogo" in *Maski,* Moscow, 1913–1914, No. 4 [cited from secondary source].

1914

Mastera baleta: ocherk istorii i teorii tantsa, St. Petersburg: N. V. Solov'ev, 1914.

"Zhizel' " in *Rech',* St. Petersburg, 4 November 1914, p. 5.

"Pakhita" in *Rech',* St. Petersburg, 2 December 1914, p. 5.

"Arlekinada" in *Rech',* St. Petersburg, 9 December 1914, p. 5.

"Benefis kordebaleta: 'Korsar' " in *Rech',* St. Petersburg, 23 December 1914, p. 5.

1915

"Pisateli na postu" in *Rech',* St. Petersburg, 30 November 1915, p. 2.

1916

"Esmeral'da" in *Rech',* St. Petersburg, 5 January 1916, p. 5.

"M. F. Kshesinskaia v 'Talismane' " in *Rech',* St. Petersburg, 19 January 1916, p. 5.

"Aragonskaia khota" in *Rech',* St. Petersburg, 8 March 1916, p. 6.

"Russkie khudozhniki-dekoratory" in *Stolitsa i usad'ba,* St. Petersburg, 1916, No. 57, pp. 4–18.

1918

Staryi i novyi balet, Petrograd: Svobodnoe iskusstvo, [1918].

"Chaikovskii v balet" in *Zhizn' iskusstva,* Petrograd, 29 October 1918, [cited from secondary source].

"Balet 'Raimonda' " in *Zhizn' iskusstva,* Petrograd, 5 November 1918, [cited from secondary source].

"Liki Erosa" in *Zhizn' iskusstva,* Petrograd, 23 November 1918, [cited from secondary source].

"Na smert' Very Karalli" in *Zhizn' iskusstva,* Petrograd, 16 December 1918, [cited from secondary source].

"Baletnye budni" in *Zhizn' iskusstva,* Petrograd, 21 December 1918 [cited from secondary source].

"Utrachennyi talisman: Benefis kordebaleta" in *Zhizn' iskusstva,* Petrograd, 25 December 1918, [cited from secondary source].

1919

Flaubert, Gustave, *Salambo,* translated by N. M. Minskii with an introduction by André Levinson, St. Petersburg, 1919, [cited from secondary source].

1920

"O 'Petrushke' Benua" in *Dom iskusstv,* Petrograd, 1920, Number 1, pp. 57–60, [cited from secondary source].

1921

"Poezdka iz Peterburga v Sibir' " in *Arkhiv Russkoi Revoliutsii,* Berlin, 1921, Volume III, pp. 190–209.

Rapport à MM. les membres du Congrès d'histoire de l'art sur la peinture française moderne dans les collections russes, Paris: J. Povolozky, 1921, [cited from secondary source].

"La litterature russe actuelle" in *La Revue mondiale,* Paris, October 1921, pp. 327–336.

"Somov" in *Zhar-Ptitsa,* Berlin, 1921, Volume 3, pp. 17–20.

"Une dernière étape des 'Ballets Russes'—*La Belle au Bois Dormant*" in *La Revue Musicale,* Paris, 1 December 1921, pp. 131–135.

"Théophile Gautier et le Ballet Romantique" in *La Revue Musicale,* Paris, 1 December 1921, pp. 53–66.

"Modern Russian Literature" in *Living Age,* Boston, 24 December 1921, pp. 781–787.

1922

La littérature russe actuelle: guerre, révolution, exil. Leçon d'ouverture faite à la Sorbonne le 20 mai 1922, Paris: J. Povolozky, 1922, [cited from secondary source].

"Fransis Zhamm" in *Grani*, Berlin, 1922, Volume I, pp. 233–251.

L'Oeuvre de Léon Bakst pour La Belle au Bois Dormant, Paris: De-Brunoff, 1922.

Bakst, The Story of Leon Bakst's Life, New York: Brentano's, 1922.

The Story of Leon Bakst's Life, Berlin: Alexander Kogan Publishing Company, 1922.

"Gumilev" in *Sovremennye zapiski*, Paris, 1922, Volume 9, pp. 309–315.

"Some Commonplaces on the Dance" in *Broom*, Rome, 1922, Volume 4, pp. 14–21.

"Vozvrashchenie Baksta: K vykhodu v svet polnoi monografii ego tvorchestva" in *Zhar-Ptitsa*, Berlin, 1922, Volume 9, pp. 2–5.

1923

Bakst: The Story of the Artist's Life, London: The Bayard Press, 1923.

The Designs of Léon Bakst for The Sleeping Princess, London: Benn Brothers Ltd., 1923.

Meister des balletts, Potsdam: Müller & Co., 1923.

"Dzhentl'men; Zametki o proze E. I. Zamiatina" in *Poslednie novosti*, Paris, March, 1923, [cited from secondary source].

"Stéphane Mallarmé, métaphysicien du ballet" in *La Revue Musicale*, Paris, 1 November 1923, pp. 21–33.

"Strawinsky et la danse" in *La Revue Musicale*, Paris, 1 December 1923, pp. 155–165.

"Moris Barres" in *Grani*, Berlin, 1923, Volume II, pp. 321–361.

1924

Bakst, Paris: H. Reynaud, 1924.

La danse au théâtre; esthétique et actualité mêlées, Paris: Bloud et Gay, 1924.

Grigor'ev, Boris Dmitrievich, *Faces of Russia*, Text by Louis Réau, Clare, Sheridan, André Levinson, Claude Farrere and André Antoine, London, 1924.

"Stravinsky and the Dance" in *Theatre Arts Monthly*, New York, November, 1924, pp. 741–754.

1925

"Notes sur le Ballet au XVII siècle: les Danseurs de Lully" in *La Revue Musicale*, Paris, 1 January 1925, pp. 44–55.

"The Spirit of the Classical Dance" in *Theatre Arts Monthly*, New York, March, 1925, pp. 165–177.

"The Spirit of the Spanish Dance" in *Theatre Arts Monthly*, New York, May, 1925, pp. 307–320.

1926

"Berain and the French Costume Tradition" in *Theatre Arts Monthly*, New York, March 1926, pp. 155–165.

"Crisis in the Ballets Russes" in *Theatre Arts Monthly*, New York, November 1926, pp. 785–792.

1927

Croisières: Vingt études sur des écrivains étrangers de ce temps, Paris: La Renaissance, 1927.

Noverre, Jean-Georges, *Lettres sur la danse et sur les ballets*, Introduction by André Levinson, Paris: Editions de la Tourelle, [1927].

Paul Valéry: Philosophe de la danse, Paris: La Tour d'Ivoire, 1927.

L'Art Cinématographique [in conjunction with Marcel l'Herbier, Léon Moussinac and Albert Valentin] Paris: F. Alcan, 1927, [cited from secondary source].

"Dostoievsky et le Diable" Part I, in *Nouvelles littéraires*, Paris, 26 March 1927, p. 4.

"Dostoievsky et le Diable" Part II, in *Nouvelles littéraires*, Paris, 2 April 1927, p. 9.

"The Negro dance under European eyes" in *Theatre Arts Monthly*, New York, April, 1927, pp. 282–293.

"The idea of the dance from Aristotle to Mallarmé" in *Theatre Arts Monthly*, New York, August, 1927, pp. 571–583.

1928

Anna Pavlova, Paris: Editions Grjébine et Vishgnak, 1928.

La Argentina; Essai sur la danse espagnole, Paris: Editions Chroniques du Jour, 1928.

"Adagio: Das klassische Tanz-Duett" in *Neue musik-Zeitung*, Stuttgart, Jahrg 49, Heft 7, 1928, pp. 206–209.

"Le dilemme des 'ballets russes' " in *Candide*, Paris, 5 January 1928, p. 7.

"Le père Férouelle, doyen de la danse à l'Opéra" in *Candide*, Paris, 12 January 1928, p. 7.

"Danseurs et acrobates" in *Candide*, Paris, 19 January 1928, p. 9.

"Le secret de Maria Valente" in *Candide*, Paris, 26 January 1928, p. 7.

"Concerts de dense" in *Candide*, Paris, 2 February 1928, p. 8.

"Un duel chorégraphique" in *Candide*, Paris, 9 February 1928, p. 7.

"Avons-nous un répertoire de danse?" in *Candide*, Paris, 16 February 1928, p. 8.

"Musique de danse" in *Candide*, Paris, 23 February 1928, p. 8.

"The anatomy of a sylph: concerning the beauty of Marie Taglioni" in *Theatre Arts Monthly*, New York, March, 1928, pp. 191–198.

"Rites orientaux, rontes rustiques" in *Candide*, Paris, 1 March 1928, p. 8.

"Hommage à Argentina; Ballets Romanoff; Djemil Anik" in *Candide*, Paris, 8 March 1928, p. 8.

"Charmes et Sortilèges" in *Candide*, Paris, 15 March 1928, p. 9.

"Le théâtre russe en deuil" in *Candide*, Paris, 22 March 1928, p. 9.

"Batterie" in *Candide*, Paris, 29 March 1928, p. 9.

"Miniatures et bibelots" in *Candide*, Paris, 5 April 1928, p. 9.

"Les faux ballets russes" in *Candide*, Paris, 12 April 1928, p. 9.

"Technique et fantaisie" in *Candide*, Paris, 19 April 1928, p. 9.

"Les plumes de paon" in *Candide*, Paris, 26 April 1928, p. 9.

"Adieux de Mlle Schwarz" in *Candide*, Paris, 3 May 1928, p. 9.

"Galas espagnols" in *Candide*, Paris, 10 May 1928, p. 9.

"La Pavlova" in *Candide*, Paris, 17 May 1928, p. 9.

"Pavlova et le ballet français" in *Candide*, Paris, 24 May 1928, p. 13.

"Léonide Leonoff et le roman russe en Russie" in *Nouvelles littéraires*, Paris, 28 May 1928, p. 6.

"La tragédie de Salomé" in *Candide*, Paris, 31 May 1928, p. 9.

"Ibsen Today" in *Living Age*, Boston, June 1928, pp. 937–942.

"Les Sakharoff 'speechs' " in *Candide*, Paris, 7 June 1928, p. 11.

"Edmund Gosse" in *Nouvelles littéraires*, Paris, 9 June 1928, p. 7.

"Aux 'Ballets Russes': Ode" in *Candide*, Paris, 14 June 1928, p. 11.

"Apollon-Musagète" in *Candide*, Paris, 21 June 1928, p. 11.

"Abraham Mapon et la Renaissance Hebraique" in *Nouvelles littéraires*, Paris, 23 June 1928, p. 8.

"Ballets espagnols—Reso" in *Candide*, Paris, 28 June 1928, p. 11.

"Variétés" in *Candide*, Paris, 5 July 1928, p. 11.

"Le Masque et le visage de Frank Wedekind" in *Nouvelles littéraires*, Paris, 5 July 1928, p. 7.

"Au Congrès d'Essen" in *Candide*, Paris, 12 July 1928, p. 11.

"Americana" in *Candide*, Paris, 19 July 1928, p. 11.

"Joseph Conrad, est-il un écrivain français?" Part I in *Nouvelles littéraires*, Paris, 4 August 1928, p. 8.

"Projets" in *Candide,* Paris, 26 July 1928, p. 9.

"The girls" in *Theatre Arts Monthly,* New York, August, 1928, pp. 597–605.

"Les avateurs du ballet de Faust" in *Candide,* Paris, 2 August 1928, p. 9.

"Joseph Conrad, est-il un écrivain français?" Part II in *Nouvelles littéraires,* Paris, 4 August 1928, p. 8.

"La verte vieillesse de 'Coppélia' " in *Candide,* Paris, 9 August 1928, p. 11.

"Les surprises de 'Marouf' " in *Candide,* Paris, 16 August 1928, p. 9.

"Thornton Wilder et les fantômes du Pont Saint-Louis" in *Nouvelles littéraires,* Paris, 25 August 1928, p. 5.

"Le répertoire: le cas de 'Sylvia' " in *Candide,* Paris, 25 August 1928, p. 11.

"Marionettes et chansons dansées" in *Candide,* Paris, 30 August 1928, p. 9.

"Billet de Vichy" in *Candide,* Paris, 6 September 1928, p. 9.

"A Vichy" in *Candide,* Paris, 13 September 1928, p. 9.

"Les débuts de Mlle Lamballe" in *Candide,* 20 September 1928, p. 11.

"Soir de Fête" in *Candide,* Paris, 27 September 1928, p. 9.

"G. A. Borgese, romancier, ou la revanche de la critique" in *Nouvelles littéraires,* Paris, 29 September 1928, p. 7.

"Argentina" in *Theatre Arts Monthly,* New York, October 1928, pp. 739–744.

"Clair de lune" in *Candide,* Paris, 4 October 1928, p. 11.

"Upton Sinclair, romancier et propagande" in *Nouvelles littéraires,* Paris, 6 October 1928, p. 6.

"Au Palace: 'Beauté de Paris' " in *Candide,* Paris, 11 October 1928, p. 11.

"La danse mixture" in *Candide,* Paris, 18 October 1928, p. 11.

"Le Roman et l'Histoire: Lion Feuchtwanger" in *Nouvelles littéraires,* Paris, 20 October 1928, p. 7.

"Quel dommage! . . ." in *Candide,* Paris, 25 October 1928, p. 11.

"Deux aspects du théâtre contemporain" in *Nouvelles littéraires,* Paris, 3 November 1928, p. 8.

"Quinault et Rowe" in *Candide,* Paris, 15 November 1928, p. 15.

"Selma Lagerloef et le génie ingénu" in *Nouvelles littéraires,* Paris, 17 November 1928, p. 6.

"Deuil-Parodie" in *Candide,* Paris, 22 November 1928, p. 15.

"La danse" in *Candide,* Paris, 29 November 1928, p. 15.

"Encore trois ballets" in *Candide,* Paris, 6 December 1928, p. 15.

"Sur un nouveau romancier russe: Joseph Kalinnikow" in *Nouvelles littéraires,* Paris, 8 December 1928, p. 6.

"Eclipse de lune" in *Candide,* Paris, 13 December 1928, p. 13.

"Le temple et le tréteau" in *Candide,* Paris, 20 December 1928, p. 15.

"Friedrich Gundolf, historien de la gloire" in *Nouvelles littéraires*, Paris, 22 December 1928, p. 6.

"Maquillage—Concours" in *Candide*, Paris, 27 December 1928, p. 13.

1929

Ballet Romantique, Paris: Editions de Trianon, 1929.

La Danse d'Aujourd'hui, Paris: Editions Duchartre de Van Buggenhoudt, 1929.

Figures Américaines: Dix-huit études sur des écrivains de ce temps, Paris: Victor Attinger, 1929.

Marie Taglioni, Paris: F. Alcan, 1929.

"Une chronique de temps présent par Arnold Zweig" in *Nouvelles littéraires*, Paris, 5 January 1929, p. 7.

"Ballet pyrotechnique" in *Candide*, Paris, 10 January 1929, p. 15.

"Leçon de choses" in *Candide*, Paris, 17 January 1929, p. 11.

"Barcelone et Seville" in *Candide*, 24 January 1929, p. 11.

"Un Maitre de la biographie: Lytton Strachey" in *Nouvelles littéraires*, Paris, 26 January 1929, p. 6.

"Rentree de Fokine" in *Candide*, Paris, 31 January 1929, p. 11.

"The Modern Dance in Germany" in *Theatre Arts Monthly*, New York, February, 1929, pp. 143–153.

"Un virtuose désabusé" in *Candide*, Paris, 7 February 1929, p. 13.

"Pas de basque" in *Candide*, Paris, 14 February 1929, p. 13.

"Elisabeth et Essex vus par Lytton Strachey" in *Nouvelles littéraires*, Paris, 16 February 1929, p. 6.

"Les intermèdes des 'Troyens' " in *Candide*, Paris, 21 February 1929, p. 11.

"Cendrillon au bal" in *Candide*, Paris, 28 February 1929, p. 11.

"Révolution et littérature" in *Nouvelles litteraires*, Paris, 2 March 1929, p. 6.

"La sphère et le cercle" in *Candide*, Paris, 7 March 1929, p. 13.

"Enfantines" in *Candide*, Paris, 14 March 1929, p. 13.

"Un romancier américain: Ludwig Lewisohn" in *Nouvelles littéraires*, Paris, 16 March 1929, p. 6.

"Matinée perdue, soirée bien finie" in *Candide*, Paris, 21 March 1929, p. 13.

"Jackson contre Jackson" in *Candide*, Paris, 28 March 1929, p. 13.

"La mission poétique et théâtrale de Hofmannsthal" in *Nouvelles littéraires*, Paris, 30 March 1929, p. 6.

"La bourreio d'Obernho" in *Candide*, Paris, 4 April 1929, p. 13.

"Nina Payne" in *Candide*, Paris, 11 April 1929, p. 11.

"Leonhard Frank, le réfractaire sentimental" in *Nouvelles littéraires*, Paris, 13 April 1929, p. 6.

"Concerts de danse" in *Candide*, Paris, 18 April 1929, p. 15.

"Lisa Duncan" in *Candide*, Paris, 25 April 1929, p. 13.

"La tragédie de Sacco et Vanzetti par Upton Sinclair" in *Nouvelles littéraires*, Paris, 27 April 1929, p. 6.

"Premieres danseuses" in *Candide*, Paris, 2 May 1929, p. 13.

"Métamorphose d'un genre" in *Candide*, Paris, 9 May 1929, p. 11.

" 'Garde blanche,' chronique de la guerre civile" in *Nouvelles litteraires*, Paris, 11 May 1929, p. 6.

"Inflation rhythmique" in *Candide*, Paris, 16 May 1929, p. 13.

"L'Ecran des demoiselles" in *Candide*, Paris, 23 May 1929, p. 13.

"Le Juif errant chez l'oncle Sam" in *Nouvelles littéraires*, Paris, 25 May 1929, p. 6.

"Semaine russe" in *Candide*, Paris, 30 May 1929, p. 11.

"Italiens et Espagnols" in *Candide*, Paris, 6 June 1929, p. 13.

"A l'ouest rien de nouveau—Menaces à l'est" in *Nouvelles littéraires*, Paris, 8 June 1929, p. 6.

"Exotismes américains" in *Candide*, Paris, 20 June 1929, p. 11.

"La 'Trilogie de la ferme espagnole' ou les brittaniques en France" in *Nouvelles littéraires*, Paris, 22 June 1929, p. 6.

"Grecs et barbares" in *Candide*, Paris, 27 June 1929, p. 15.

"Jacques Copeau devant l'opinion étrangère" in *Nouvelles littéraires*, Paris, 6 July 1929, p. 12.

"Autour des 'Frères Karamazoff' Dostoievsky et George Sand" in *Nouvelles littéraires*, Paris, 13 July 1929, p. 8.

"Complainte d'*Igor*" in *Candide*, Paris, 18 July 1929, p. 11.

"Gala d'été" in *Candide*, Paris, 25 July 1929, p. 11.

"La 'Tyrolienne' de Rossini" in *Candide*, 1 August 1929, p. 11.

"Miss Florence—Sophismes et vérités" in *Candide*, Paris, 8 August 1929, p. 11.

"Encore les 'Oiseaux Noirs' " in *Candide*, Paris, 15 August 1929, p. 11.

"Les origines de la guerre: un pamphlet d'Emil Ludwig" in *Nouvelles littéraires*, Paris, 17 August 1929, p. 6.

"Le ballet de 'Romeo' " in *Candide*, Paris, 22 August 1929, p. 11.

"Le tombeau de Diaghilew" in *Candide*, Paris, 29 August 1929, p. 11.

"Aframérique" in *Nouvelles littéraires*, Paris, 31 August 1929, p. 6.

"The Modern Dance in Germany" in *Theatre Arts Monthly*, New York, September, 1929, pp. 143–153.

"The Nature of the Cinema" in *Theatre Arts Monthly*, New York, September, 1929, pp. 684–693.

"Grande saison d'été" in *Candide*, Paris, 5 September 1929, p. 11.

"Souvenirs d'un pierrot" in *Candide*, Paris, 12 September 1929, p. 11.

"De Harlem à la Cannebière" in *Nouvelles littèraires*, Paris, 14 September 1929, p. 6.

"Lorsque l'étoile parait" in *Candide*, Paris, 19 September 1929, p. 11.

"Le cas de Mlle Spessivtzeva" in *Candide*, Paris, 26 September 1929, p. 13.

"Cholokoff et son épopée cosaque" in *Nouvelles littéraires*, Paris, 28 September 1929, p. 6.

"Rondes populaires" in *Candide*, Paris, 3 October 1929, p. 11.

"Chez Mayol—A Mogador" in *Candide*, Paris, 10 October 1929, p. 11.

"Un échec—Un succès" in *Candide*, Paris, 17 October 1929, p. 14.

"Jacob Wasserman et le procès de la Justice" in *Nouvelles littéraires*, Paris, 19 October 1929, p. 6.

"Cinéchorégraphie" in *Candide*, Paris, 24 October 1929, p. 13.

"Résurrection" in *Candide*, Paris, 31 October 1929, p. 13.

"Un philosophe mystérieux: N. Fédoroff et son projet de résurrection des morts" in *Nouvelles littéraires*, 2 November 1929, p. 6.

"Epilogue—Cendrillon" in *Candide*, Paris, 7 November 1929, p. 12.

"Recital et Parade" in *Candide*, Paris, 14 November 1929, p. 12.

"Le roman d'une génération: 'Barbara' de Franz Werfel" in *Nouvelles littéraires*, Paris, 16 November 1929, p. 6.

"Rentrée de Sakharoff" in *Candide*, Paris, 21 November 1929, p. 13.

"L'Art de tourner" in *Candide*, Paris, 28 November 1929, p. 14.

"Opinions et propos de Thomas Mann" in *Nouvelles littéraires*, Paris, 30 November 1929, p. 6.

"La rentrée de Borlin" in *Candide*, Paris, 5 December 1929, p. 15.

"Expressionisme" in *Candide*, Paris, 12 December 1929, p. 13.

"Un immoraliste vertueux: D. H. Lawrence" in *Nouvelles littéraires*, Paris, 14 December 1929, p. 6.

"La danse à travers les pays et les livres" in *L'Art vivant*, Paris, 15 December 1929, pp. 989–990.

"Djemil-Anik et les sortilèges malais" in *Candide*, Paris, 19 December 1929, p. 15.

"Vedettes et débutantes" in *Candide*, Paris, 26 December 1929, p. 12.

1930

Marie Taglioni, translated by Cyril W. Beaumont, London: Imperial Society of Teachers of Dancing, 1930.

"Prométhée à l'Opéra" in *Candide*, Paris, 9 January 1930, p. 12.

"Ford Madox Ford et sa tétralogie" in *Nouvelles littéraires*, Paris, 11 January 1930, p. 6.

"Gambades et Pomiès" in *Candide*, Paris, 16 January 1930, p. 13.

"A la mémoire de Marie Petipa" in *Candide*, Paris, 23 January 1930, p. 13.

"Le chevalier, la mort et le diable" in *Nouvelles littéraires*, Paris, 25 January 1930, p. 6.

"Ballet de Vera Nemtchinova" in *Candide*, Paris, 30 January 1930, p. 11.

"Rentrée de Térésina" in *Candide*, Paris, 6 February 1930, p. 13.

"Divertissements" in *Candide*, Paris, 13 February 1930, p. 13.

"V. Sirine et son joueur d'échecs" in *Nouvelles littéraires*, Paris, 15 February 1930, p. 6.

"Le grand Prix de l'Opéra" in *Candide*, Paris, 20 February 1930, p. 13.

"Bagatelles laborieuses" in *Candide*, Paris, 27 February 1930, p. 13.

"Alfred Doeblin, romancier d'élan vital" in *Nouvelles littéraires*, Paris, 1 March 1930, p. 6.

"Max Brod, romancier du coup de foudre" in *Nouvelles littéraires*, Paris, 15 March 1930, p. 6.

"Le beau Danube Bleu" in *Candide*, Paris, 27 March 1930, p. 13.

"Un livre euraméricain, le 'Lincoln' d'Emil Ludwig" in *Nouvelles littéraires*, Paris, 29 March 1930, p. 6.

"Grotesques" in *Candide*, Paris, 3 April 1930, p. 13.

"La danse" in *Candide*, Paris, 10 April 1930, p. 13.

"Manuel Galvez et son Iliade argentine" in *Nouvelles littéraires*, Paris, 12 April 1930, p. 6.

"Narcisse et Chérubin" in *Candide*, Paris, 17 April 1930, p. 15.

"Choses d'Espagne" in *Candide*, Paris, 24 April 1930, p. 13.

"L'Esprit et les formes de la danse javanaise" in *L'Art vivant*, Paris, 1 May 1930, pp. 367–369, 371.

"Combats japonais" in *Candide*, Paris, 22 May 1930, p. 13.

"L'Opera Russe et Lisa Duncan" in *Candide*, Paris, 29 May 1930, p. 13.

"La poésie chez les Soviets: le suicide de Mayakovsky" in *Nouvelles littéraires*, Paris, 31 May 1930, p. 6.

"Semaine française" in *Candide*, Paris, 5 June 1930, p. 13.

"Echecs et tarots" in *Candide*, Paris, 12 June 1930, p. 12.

"Faux départ; entrée opportune" in *Candide*, 19 June 1930, p. 13.

"Gala espagnol et Ballet d'Opéra" in *Candide*, Paris, 26 June 1930, p. 13.

"Révérences et fanfreluches" in *Candide*, Paris, 3 July 1930, p. 13.

"Feu de paille" in *Candide*, Paris, 10 July 1930, p. 11.

"Sir Arthur Conan Doyle et la gloire de Sherlock Holmes" in *Nouvelles littéraires*, Paris, 12 July 1930, p. 6.

"Rêlache" in *Candide*, Paris, 17 July 1930, p. 13.

"Championne de France" in *Candide*, Paris, 24 July 1930, p. 12.

"La première femme de Dostoievsky" Part I, in *Nouvelles littéraires*, Paris, 26 July 1930, p. 6.

"Observations astronomiques" in *Candide*, Paris, 31 July 1930, p. 11.

"La première femme de Dostoievsky" Part II, in *Nouvelles littéraires*, Paris, 2 August 1930, p. 6.

"Les périls de la 'Péri' " in *Candide*, Paris, 7 August 1930, p. 11.

"E. Gordon Craig, 'l'Homme qui n'a rien fait' " in *Nouvelles littéraires,* Paris, 23 August 1930, p. 6.

"Ravel à Vichy" in *Candide,* Paris, 18 September 1930, p. 11.

"Edna Ferber et le romanesque américain" in *Nouvelles littéraires,* Paris, 27 September 1930, p. 6.

"Adage à quatre" in *Candide,* Paris, 9 October 1930, p. 13.

"Bacchanale de 'Tannhaeuser' " in *Candide,* Paris, 16 October 1930, p. 12.

"Histoire naturelle de la bête humaine" in *Nouvelles littéraires,* Paris, 18 October 1930, p. 6.

"Virginia Zucchi" in *Candide,* Paris, 30 October 1930, p. 13.

"La Divine Lady et la Ronde des Statues" in *Le Figaro Artistique,* Paris, November 1930, pp. 32–33.

"Le Ruban de Velours noir ou Degas chorégraphe" in *Le Figaro Artistique,* Paris, November 1930, pp. 10–15.

"Americana" in *Candide,* Paris, 6 November 1930, p. 13.

"Mirages d'Orient" in *Candide,* Paris, 13 November 1930, p. 15.

"L'Allemagne de 1930 vue à travers les livres" Part I, in *Nouvelles littéraires,* Paris, 15 November 1930, p. 6.

"Javanese dancing: the spirit and the form" in *Theatre Arts Monthly,* New York, December 1930, pp. 1056–1065.

"L'Allemagne de 1930 vue à traverse les livres" Part II, in *Nouvelles littéraires,* Paris, 6 December 1930, p. 6.

"Rentrée de 'Petrouchka' " in *Candide,* Paris, 18 December 1930, p. 15.

"L'Allemagne de 1930 vue à travers les livres" Part III, in *Nouvelles littéraires,* Paris, 20 December 1930, p. 6.

1931

La Vie Pathétique de Dostoievsky, Paris: Plon, 1931.

"L'Allemagne de 1930 vue à travers les livres" Part IV, in *Nouvelles littéraires,* Paris, 3 January 1931, p. 6.

"Le désordre allemand" in *Candide,* Paris, 15 January 1931, p. 11.

"L'Allemagne de 1930 vue à travers les livres" Part V in *Nouvelles littéraires,* Paris, 24 January 1931, p. 6.

"Le génie d'Anna Pavlova" in *Candide,* Paris, 29 January 1931, p. 13.

"Nouveaux ballets russes" in *Candide,* Paris, 12 February 1931, p. 13.

"Romans parallèles: du 'Fleuve sotj' de Léonoff à la 'Volga' de Pilniak" in *Nouvelles litteraires,* Paris, 28 February 1931, p. 6.

"Serge Lifar à l'Opéra" in *Candide,* Paris, 12 March 1931, p. 13.

"Sigmund Freud vu par Stefan Zweig" in *Nouvelles littéraires,* Paris, 21 March 1931, p. 6.

"L'Angleterre nouvelle: Histoire de chasse de souvenirs de guerre" in *Nouvelles littéraires,* Paris, 4 April 1931, p. 6.

"Harmonies et dissonances" in *Candide,* Paris, 9 April 1931, p. 11.

"I. H. M. Tomlinson et le roman maritime" in *Nouvelles littéraires,* Paris, 9 May 1931, p. 6.

"Sur un air de Sardane" in *Candide,* Paris, 14 May 1931, p. 13.

"J. B. Priestley et le retour à Dickens" in *Nouvelles littéraires,* Paris, 23 May 1931, p. 6.

"A l'Opéra: 'Bacchus et Ariane' " in *Candide,* Paris, 28 May 1931, p. 13.

"Occident et Orient" in *Candide,* Paris, 4 June 1931, p. 12.

"Jacob Wassermann et la jeunesse d'aujourd'hui" in *Nouvelles littéraires,* Paris, 27 June 1931, p. 6.

"*Amphion* aux ballets Ida Rubinstein" in *Candide,* Paris, 2 July 1931, p. 13.

"Les 'Portraits en miniature' de Lytton Strachey" in *Nouvelles littéraires,* Paris, 18 July 1931, p. 6.

"Les danseurs de Bali" in *Candide,* Paris, 30 July 1931, p. 10.

"Où en est en France la danse theatrale?" in *Candide,* Paris, 3 September 1931, p. 11.

"Va-t-on réformer l'enseignement de la danse?" in *Candide,* Paris, 24 September 1931, p. 10.

"Au coin de feu avec Gordon Craig" in *Candide,* Paris, 8 October 1931, p. 13.

"L'Habit qui fait le moine" in *Candide,* Paris, 22 October 1931, p. 12.

"Ballets français" in *Candide,* Paris, 19 November 1931, p. 15.

"Livrets de ballets" in *Candide,* Paris, 17 December 1931, p. 15.

1932

Loutchansky, Paris: Editions Le Triangle, 1932.

"La Revanche de l'Ecole" in *Candide,* Paris, 14 January 1932, p. 15.

"Résurrection de 'Giselle' " in *Candide,* Paris, 11 February 1932, p. 13.

"De 'Giselle' au 'Spectre de la rose' " in *Candide,* Paris, 10 March 1932, p. 11.

"Germany's Literary Revenge" in *Living Age,* Boston, April 1932, pp. 163–167.

"Métamorphoses" in *Candide,* Paris, 7 April 1932, p. 13.

"Rentrée de la rhythmique" in *Candide,* Paris, 5 May 1932, p. 13.

"Reflets d'Allemagne . . . et de Perse" in *Candide,* Paris, 2 June 1932, p. 13.

"Rentrée d'Argentina" in *Candide,* Paris, 9 June 1932, p. 13.

"Le concours de danse" in *Candide,* Paris, 30 June 1932, p. 12.
"La danse" in *Candide,* Paris, 14 July 1932, p. 14.

1933

Les Visages de la danse, Paris: B. Grasset, [1933].
"O nekotorykh chertakh tvorchestva S. S. Iushkevicha" in *Sem' dnei,*
    Paris, 1933, Volume 255, pp. 83–95 [cited from secondary source].

1934

Serge Lifar, destin d'un danseur, Paris: B. Grasset, [1934].

1943

Dostoievsky, vida dolorosa, translated by Fabian Casares, Buenos Aires,
    1943.

1946

Cartas sobre la danza y sobre los ballets [por] Juan Jorge Noverre, prece-
    didas por una biografía del autor por Andrés Levinson, trad. Susana
    Uriburu, Buenos Aires [1946].

1971

Bakst, the Story of the Artist's Life, New York: B. Blom, 1971.
The Designs of Leon Bakst for "The Sleeping Princess," New York: B.
    Blom, 1971.

1977

Marie Taglioni, translated by Cyril W. Beaumont, London: Dance Books
    Ltd., 1977.
"André Levinson on Isadora Duncan", introduction by Jill Silverman, in
    Ballet Review, New York, Volume 6, Number 4, 1977–1978, pp.
    1–20.

1980

"The Two Sacres", translated by Deborah Loft, in *New Performance,* San
    Francisco, 1980, Volume II, Number 1, pp. 19–21.

Index